Surrounded
by
Geniuses

Unlocking Brilliance in Yourself,
Your Colleagues and Your Organization

Dr. Alan S. Gregerman

SOURCEBOOKS, INC.®
NAPERVILLE, ILLINOIS

Published by Sourcebooks, Inc.
P.O. Box 4410, Naperville, Illinois 60567-4410
(630) 961-3900
Fax: (630) 961-2168
www.sourcebooks.com

Library of Congress Cataloging-in-Publication Data

Gregerman, Alan S.
  Surrounded by geniuses : unlocking the brilliance in your organization and your people / Alan S. Gregerman.
     p. cm.
  ISBN 978-1-4022-0910-9 (hardcover)
  1. Success in business--United States. 2. Customer services--United States. 3. Organizational effectiveness. 4. Public relations--United States. 5. Leadership--United States. I. Title.

HF5386.G767 2007
658.4'09--dc22
                                                          2007010915

Printed and bound in the United States of America.
BG 10 9 8 7 6 5 4 3 2 1

To Lisa, Sara, Carly and Noah—
you make every journey a source of wonder and possibilities.

And to everyone who believes there is a better way
to do the things that matter most.

Contents

How the slowest swimmers in the world came to dominate the world of swimming, and why you don't have to be brilliant to do brilliant things.

Why you have to reinvent the game if you want to win.

Why traditional approaches to strategy, innovation, and marketing no longer make any sense and what to do about it.

Why our innate gift for curiosity is the only real weapon in the battle to remain relevant and how to rediscover it; and

Why geography matters, and why a thirteenth-century traveler might be the most important business thinker of the twenty-first century.

What if we could make and deliver on a promise that really mattered?
A journey back in time to meet a man with bad feet, a reasonable idea and a powerful promise...
(Leon Leonwood Bean)

What if we could create more meaningful conversations?
A journey through the neighborhood with a nine-year-old girl, a box of cookies and the magic of a recurring conversation...
(The Girl Scouts)

What if we could create a performance filled with wonder and possibilities?
A journey under a tent where the concept of a circus has been reinvented...
(Cirque du Soleil)

What if we could solve practically any request no matter how difficult?
A journey into the lobby of one of the world's great hotels and a day in the life of a world-class concierge...
(The Ritz Carlton on Central Park)

Preface

Greetings and welcome to *Surrounded by Geniuses,* a book about the real potential that each of us, and the companies and organizations we work in, has to accomplish new and brilliant things. . .even if we haven't ever done them before.

To set the stage, let me start with a couple of essential questions. Asking questions is at the heart of this book and the key to unlocking new ideas and delivering greater value to customers.

First:

How many times have you arrived at work, exchanged greetings with your colleagues, conversed at the coffeepot or water cooler, attended a meeting or two, and then sat down at your desk overcome by the incredible feeling that you were *surrounded by geniuses?* If you're like most people, the answer is "never." In fact, when asked in a large group, this simple question causes most people in companies and organizations to laugh hysterically.

Second:

How many times have you left work, climbed into your car or boarded a bus or train, then looked around and been struck with an awesome sense that you were surrounded by a world of geniuses and *brilliant ideas*? If you're like most people and companies caught up in the pressures and routines of day-to-day life, the answer is also "never." In fact, as you take the journey home, you're more likely to see a world filled with aggressive drivers, total (or partial) idiots, and mindless advertisements than sources of great inspiration.

Yet as funny as these two questions might sound, they are at the heart of what it takes for companies and organizations of all kinds to innovate, grow, and succeed in difficult times. In a world that constantly rewards new and better ideas, we must all find ways to consistently deliver greater value to the customers and stakeholders we choose to serve. And we can only do this by unlocking the everyday genius in ourselves, our coworkers, and our partners. It sounds like a tall order, but it's hardly impossible. In fact, our work with leading organizations in many industries over the past twenty years has shown that all of us have the ability, under the right circumstances, to make a real difference in small and large ways—not by doing business as usual or by sitting around a conference table brainstorming until a breakthrough occurs or our brains explode, but by working together to tackle the world around us head on *and* seeing it as a place already filled with brilliant ideas, unlimited sources of inspiration, and endless possibilities that can be used to transform our companies, organizations, the lives of our customers, and even ourselves.

This straightforward notion is the heart of this book, and the implications are staggering. It suggests that the world we all share is very different than the one we shared even ten years ago and the one that most business thinking is still based on. In today's world, not only is the inspiration to do remarkable things everywhere, but also all of us have access to essentially the same knowledge; every company has a real chance to win even if it wasn't winning before; every employee has the ability to make a real difference even if they haven't done so before; and the most curious and curiously creative people and organizations will likely be the ones that survive. Welcome to a world in which we are all literally and figuratively *surrounded by geniuses!*

So the challenge we all face is very different than we might have imagined, and the reason for optimism should be much greater. With the possible exception of those relatively rare fields in which a high level of specialized technical expertise is an essential part of the equation, most companies and organizations will sink or swim based on their ability to reinvent the experience they deliver to their customers. And the insight and inspiration to do that are all around us. So stop laughing and round up the geniuses you work with. It's time to get off our bottoms and head out on a journey—or ten journeys—to the future of customer and business success . . .

Introduction

Where should we begin? In this book, I hope to show how you and your company or organization can win in the most competitive markets. Not by doing business as usual, but by rediscovering the curiosity and talent in all of us and using it to unlock genius in the world around us.

What Is "Genius?"

Before we get started, let's spend a few moments thinking about what it means to be a genius. Then let's think about why it is imperative for all of our organizations to be brilliant. After that, we will take a quick detour into a typical workplace to find out why it's so hard to come up with ideas that really make a difference.

As I hope you gathered from the Preface, this book is based on two important ideas that have powerful implications for you and your company or organization.

The first idea is that we all have the potential to be geniuses. This is probably not in the way we think about the greatest minds in history. After all, people such as Confucius, Ptolemy, Leonardo da Vinci, Thomas Edison, Madame Curie, and Albert Einstein were exceedingly clever and not likely to be found hanging out by the coffeemaker in your office. But we can be geniuses in a way that matters far more to our success. In fact, each of us has the ability to be purposefully brilliant—by working together to bring fresh perspectives to pressing problems, by discovering new and better ways of doing things, and by delivering greater value for the customers who count on us each and every day. All we have to do is look at ourselves and each other a bit differently. To be geniuses, we simply need the right insight and the right circumstances.

The second idea is that we live in a world where we are surrounded by genius and knowledge that can be used to transform practically any company or organization. This is probably not in the way that we tend to think about great ideas, the process of coming up with them, or the cast of characters involved. After all, most of us don't own a lab coat, let alone hang out in state-of-the-art laboratories filled with Ph.D. scientists, super computers busy crunching the most complex algorithms, or Petri dishes filled with the latest slices of DNA. But "genius" in a way that matters far more to our success. The most relevant labs for most of our purposes are probably bustling city streets, quiet mountain trails, days at the zoo, nights at the circus, visits to local museums, hours spent watching countless reruns of award-winning television sitcoms, silly contests made up just for fun, or a somewhat systematic excursion to the best practices of a set of totally unrelated organizations and industries. In fact, to succeed consistently, we would have to be open to putting ourselves in places filled with possibilities that are often unfamiliar or at least unexpected. Places that actually have the potential to bring out the genius in us. All we would have to do is look at the world differently. To discover genius, we simply need the right insight and the right circumstances.

The Failure of a First Glance

The only problem with these two ideas is the reality that they run counter to the way most of us—and most of our organizations—prefer to view each other and the world around us. They run counter to the insight we receive and the "circumstances" that most of us find ourselves in as leaders, employees, team members, and adults. But how?

First, most of us tend to think of our colleagues and ourselves as cogs in a wheel that is presumably intended to keep our organizations moving forward. We are the pieces of a puzzle that rarely know what the final picture will look like, let alone what we can do to make it more remarkable. So when asked about our coworkers we are apt to reply: *"Joe works in finance"; "Jane is in human resources"; "Carlos is a sales guy";* or *"Helene holds down the fort in the records department."* With the exception of our closest friends at work, coworkers are roles and responsibilities, job titles, and the inhabitants of certain offices, cubes, or places out in the plant. They are somewhere on a chart called "organization," in a box defined by their duties rather than their unique talents. If we work in a large company or organization, that "somewhere" and those "duties" are more likely to be very specific. But their unique talents are more likely to be unknown, which means that our collective talents, the true assets of our organization, are likely to be untapped.

And their behavior, for the most part, supports our simple notions. Either perched behind or surrounded by a few personal effects, they dutifully try to get their job done by moving things ahead, checking off essential items on their "to do" lists, tackling each day's most necessary and unnecessary phone calls, sending out critical e-mails, attending their share of important and unimportant meetings, and putting out the most threatening fires. They rarely ever come out to play—if "play" means singing, dancing, laughing, or launching a mighty barrage of creative ideas into the hallway of our unexpecting universe. And they probably aren't racing in and out of the building looking for ways to make the organization better.

And our behavior, for the most part, allows them to get away with it. As long as they get their tasks done—and don't mess with our most sacred stuff—we seem quite content to have them around. After all, it would be very lonely without them. Besides, we share the same ultimate objective of making it through the day unharmed. So we can't imagine that they would be waiting for the moment to be brilliant. In our eyes, they are more likely to be waiting for the moment to leave work a bit early. With each day that passes, we are less likely to discover something remarkable about them that could, if unlocked, help us to be a better company or organization. No wonder the notion of being surrounded by geniuses is so hard to fathom.

We certainly can't imagine our organizations being brilliant either. After all, aren't they simply the sum total of these average people being guided by a group of leaders who are trying desperately not to lose their jobs? Leaders whose own ambitions are tied to making modest changes…not to betting the ranch on a new or unfamiliar idea? Who cares if our business or organization actually began its life by doing something brilliant? Let's be slightly better this year than we were last year. We can do that with incremental thinking or by quickly copying a competitor's newest idea. Stay close to our industry and our knowledge base, because fresh thinking breeds contempt but familiarity breeds success.

Not any longer.

Daring to Talk with Strangers

What if we looked differently at people, organizations, and the world around us? What if we saw them as a remarkable set of assets that could be combined to do something brilliant? What if we actually assumed that our coworkers were geniuses in hiding, eagerly waiting for the opportunity to jump out of their seats and their roles to make a difference? What if we actually expected them to create everyday breakthroughs that would move us way ahead of the competition? And what if we believed that everyone actually came to work each day hoping to make a difference? Then, with the right insight and circumstances, almost anything might be possible.

And what if we saw the richness of the world around us in a different light? What if we understood that the only way to discover very different ideas was to look in very different places?

But how do we "relearn" to look at each other, our organizations, and the world we share through a different set of eyes after all these years of trying not to? If you read my book *Lessons from the Sandbox,* you know that I spend a lot of time learning from children and trying to figure out how to apply their natural gifts to our world as adults, companies, and organizations. When we were kids, we saw things differently. We didn't have preconceived notions about ourselves, each other, or the world around us. Every day we engaged the world with passion, energy, fresh eyes, and a compelling sense of wonder, curiosity, and honesty. We saw in each other the chance to learn new things, new games, and new skills. In the simplest things around us, we imagined virtually endless possibilities. We took ideas from one place and brought them over to another. While our worlds were relatively small, they were also immense—offering a seemingly endless assortment of things to explore, understand, and apply to whatever mattered most.

But somewhere between the sandbox and the world of adult work, most of us lost the knack for seeing each other and the world around us as the rich soil for unlocking new ideas and opportunities . . .and for delivering different and greater value to our customers. As we grew older, we began to see people for what they appeared to be rather than what they could be. We began to see things and even ideas for what they appeared to be in the context in which we found them, rather than what they could be in a new context that we could create for them.

Imagine my amusement not long ago when I walked our daughter Carly, who was eight years old at the time, to the bus stop to head off to school. As we passed a person I had never seen in our neighborhood, someone who looked a bit suspicious through the lens of my overly protective parental eyes, I cautioned her to avoid talking to strangers. It is something most of our parents told us as kids, and it seems even more important today in our less than certain world. "But, Papa," she replied with real honesty and a bit of confusion, "how will I ever make new friends? And how will I ever learn new things?"

And, I might add, how will she and her new friends ever grow up to reinvent the companies, organizations, and world they will be part of someday? Breaking the chains of everyday genius is a challenge for all of us as grown-ups—even those of us who spend our lives helping others to come up with new ideas. Maybe I need a better way to be optimistic in the face of possibilities and caution.

Having said these things, I must admit that this is a book about talking to strangers and putting ourselves in places filled with uncertainty and possibilities. And then it's about making the most out of those possibilities. "Be open, curious, and cautious" is sound advice for business and organizational travelers, too. Not everything out there is a source of great ideas for you and your company or organizations. But there is a lot more worth exploring and understanding than you might have ever imagined. Every day we walk right past ideas that could change our lives and the lives of those we choose to serve, but we refuse to let them catch our attention.

Seeing a World of Possibilities

Before I leave the notion of thinking and acting with the openness of a child, let me share one more scene that might help to frame our challenge as adults and organizations. It is a scene that stuck in my mind as I was writing this book. A couple of years ago, I took our son, Noah, who was four at the time, for his very first eye exam. As we all know, first times are often filled with concern and curiosity. On the way there, he asked a lot of questions. Many of them were about the details of the procedure, but some showed his real concern for somebody messing with his eyes.

"Are they going to touch my eyeballs or put sticky, slimy stuff in them?" he wondered aloud.

"No way," I replied. "The doctor just wants you to look through some really cool glasses to find out how well you can see."

"That's all?" Noah asked.

"That's all!" I responded.

"Okay, let's do it."

So we arrived, waited for our turn, and then got comfortably aligned in the examination chair, which itself was a source of more questions and endless possibilities. Then the doctor entered the exam room, said hello, gave her take on why we had called this meeting, and asked Noah if he could read the letters on the top line of the eye chart. Realizing that the chart with pictures was better, the following conversation ensued:

Doctor: "Let's start with the top picture."

Noah: "That's a sailboat."

Doctor: "Good. Let's try the next row . . ."

Noah: "An 'O' and an 'X.'"

Doctor: "Very good. Let's try the next row . . ."

Noah: "A flag, star, heart."

Doctor: "Great. And the next row . . ."

Noah: "An 'O', sailboat, star, teacup, another 'X.'"

Doctor: "Let's try one more row. What is this?"

Noah: "A dot."

Doctor: "It's something a bit different than a dot. Want to try again?"

Noah: "A very little dot."

Doctor: "Let's try once more. It's actually a common shape."

Noah (after a pause to think a bit): "A spaceship."

Doctor: "Not exactly."

Noah (after another pause): "Is it a monster truck crushing a car?"

Doctor: "Does it look like anything else?"

Noah: "A dog in a monster truck crushing a car."

Doctor: "Not exactly, but that's good enough for now."

In fact (or in the world of adult facts), it was another teacup, but a much smaller teacup. In reality, it was a source of frustration for Noah and the doctor. Yet it could have been a moment of possibilities. As Noah approached the limits of what he could see clearly, he achieved the *start* of his imagination while the doctor reached the *limits* of her imagination.

So it is with most adults, companies, and organizations. We seem preoccupied with seeing the limits of who we are, what we know, and what we need to know. Rarely do we commit to reaching the start of our individual and collective imaginations.

As a result, although we are capable of taking a fresh and powerful look at the possibilities around us, we rarely ever do. As adults and organizations, our greatest challenge and our greatest opportunity is to see ourselves and the world differently. We need to see teacups as spaceships or as dogs in monster trucks running over cars. We need to find the second or third possibility. We need to stop choosing to see things just the way they are and start imagining the way that they could be.

The Real Challenge for Leaders

If there is another big idea in this book, it is the notion that most leaders can't lead. Not if leading means getting a group of *ordinary* people to achieve *extraordinary* results. If they could, leaders would spend a lot less time whining about the world around them—and the lack of creativity, enthusiasm, and initiative of their employees—and a lot more time creating the context for genius to occur. Challenging times, it seems, have forced them to be preoccupied with short-term objectives and the numbers at any cost rather than the power of people to make the right things happen. We'll think about this in detail in a little while.

First, in Part I, let's set the stage by seeing why people, companies, and organizations have so much trouble being brilliant. Then in Part II, we'll head out on ten journeys to places and ideas that could transform your business. In Part III, we'll figure out how to use these ideas to turn your organization into a veritable engine of innovation and customer value.

Here are just a couple of quick notes. Throughout this book, I will be using the words "company" and "organization" somewhat interchangeably to identify the places where you and your colleagues hang out. I recognize that readers come from a wide variety of places and these words are meant to encompass the great diversity of organizations where you might work in the private, public, and community sectors. Although I spend most of my time working with corporations, I hope that those of you who do not work specifically in companies will still see the relevance of these ideas to your world. I also use the word "customer" to identify the people and organizations we choose to serve. While some government and nonprofit organizations, and even some corporations and professional service firms, do not use the word "customer," again I hope you will understand that my intention is to focus on our ability as organizations to deliver the most compelling value to those we serve—whether we think of them as customers, citizens, members, associates, patients, shareholders, or clients—and to make them as successful as possible in what they are trying to accomplish.

Part One

The Context

We know what we are, but know not what we may be.
—William Shakespeare

Genius is one percent inspiration, ninety-nine
percent perspiration.
—Thomas Edison

Is it possible for companies and organizations to be brilliant consistently? For the past several years this question has intrigued and even preoccupied some of the best minds in business. So we search for excellence, try to find the difference between being great and merely good, determine what separates market leaders from the pack or any other model that will give us an edge.

Then one by one, leading companies stub their toes or, worse yet, lose their way. They begin a precipitous slide from less relevance to irrelevance. Some even disappear, first from our radar screen and then from the world of business itself. Models thought to be brilliant yesterday become old faster than ever before. Customers who were taken for granted change seemingly overnight and with them change our notions of what it means to deliver value. The half-lives of products, services, ideas, and brands that we hold dear shrink before our very eyes.

And it's not just the Big Three—Ford, General Motors, and Chrysler—who struggle to survive. World beaters like AOL and Dell rise like meteors to lead their industries and then fall back down to earth. No longer the leader of the Internet that it helped bring into nearly every home, AOL is forced to test an entirely new business model based on today's realities. Dell is now pressed by a world of new and old competitors who offer lower cost, better service, or both and by the limits of its once-perfect distribution model. Even today's hippest business realities change tomorrow. MySpace.com becomes *the* place for young people to hang out and communicate on the Web, and then twelve months later it is forced to wonder if it has quickly become overused and underappreciated.

Perfect strategies. Brilliant innovations. World-class marketing. Unbeatable formulas for success.

What's a company to do?

I can't pretend to predict the future in any specific way, so you won't find me telling you which of the remarkable companies described in this book will be leaders for the next fifty years. In fact, I assume that many of them won't be around in the years to come. There is simply too much that can go right and wrong. What I will predict is the nature of the people, companies, organizations, and ideas that will endure. That is rather simple. I'd also like to predict that you and your company or organization will be around for as long as you choose to deliver compelling value to the customers you serve.

So in Part I of this book I'm going to explain a bit more about the nature of the business world as I see it—a world filled with great challenges and even greater opportunities to do remarkable things—and I am going to suggest the reasons why we typically fail to live up to our potential and why curiosity is the one competitive weapon that is essential to our long-term survival.

Chapter One

White People Swimming Slowly

Or ...

How the slowest swimmers in the world came to dominate the world of competitive swimming—and why you don't have to be brilliant to do brilliant things.

If you watch the finals of any major international swimming competition, you are likely to see a group of predominantly white people battling for the top prizes. Very white people. About as white as white people can get. Most of them are likely northern Europeans or their descendants who swim for countries like the Netherlands, France, Germany, Poland, the United Kingdom, Canada, Russia, Sweden, the Ukraine, South Africa, Australia, the United States, and Zimbabwe. In fact, of the thirty-two gold medals awarded in swimming at the 2004 Olympic Games, twenty-eight were won by white people. The remaining four were won by swimmers from Japan and China, two countries that are beginning to break the mold.

The fact that white people dominate international swimming is not that remarkable, but the circumstances by which they came to rule the sport are. Until the late 1800s white people were possibly the slowest swimmers on the planet, and by all accounts they were clueless about how to swim fast. That is not to say they were trying to swim slowly. In fact, the finest white swimmers in this era assumed that they were really zooming along, and they had no reason to think otherwise. Then one day a harsh reality splashed them upside the head.

For those of you who don't spend a lot of time swimming or thinking about swimming (although you probably should because swimming is great exercise for people of all ages), let me interrupt our story to give you a bit of background information.

Different Swimming Strokes Matter

To start with, four basic strokes are used today in swimming competitions around the world, and each of these strokes has its own special requirements.

The first stroke is the *freestyle*, in which, as the name implies, swimmers are free to do practically anything they want to propel themselves across the pool other than push themselves off of the bottom of the pool or the lane markers. Freestyle swimmers typically do the *front crawl,* a stroke in which they remain essentially on their chests and do long overhead arm pulls combined with a rapid flutter kick. This combination is the fastest of the swimming strokes over any distance and the clear preference of every top swimmer in the freestyle. It is also what you and I would probably do if we were trying to avoid a shark, a stingray, or some other danger at the beach. But technically swimmers competing in the freestyle are allowed to do any stroke they choose, including the sidestroke, which is quite

Suddenly, in two relatively quick iterations, everyday genius had unlocked a better way to do something.

popular among retired people out for a recreational swim in the North Sea, and the dog paddle, which is quite popular among young children just learning to swim and, of course, golden and flat-coated retrievers.

The second competitive swimming stroke is the *backstroke*, in which swimmers can also do almost anything they want to propel themselves across the pool as long as they stay on their backs. Swimmers doing this stroke typically do the *back crawl*, in which they lie flat on their backs and do alternating long overhead arm pulls followed by elbow pushes combined with a flutter kick. This is my favorite stroke, as it allows me to keep my head out of the water and look around, and it makes breathing less of an effort. It is also the only stroke in which I have any chance at all of beating our kids in a race.

What if there are more brilliant ways to do things? And what if those more brilliant ways are all around us simply waiting for us to discover them?

The third stroke is the *breaststroke*, in which swimmers stay on their chests moving their arms forward and then pulling them back while barely breaking the surface of the water. This stroke is accompanied by a "frog kick," which looks like a frog's back legs as it moves through the water. The breaststroke is a great stroke for learning to swim and for open-water swimming when you need to see where you are going (especially if there are a lot of obstacles or jellyfish around). Also it lets you keep your head out of the water if you prefer, although the best competitive swimmers seem to attack the water with their faces and heads as they enter into a quick glide. However, the breaststroke is the slowest stroke in competitive swimming and requires a lot of energy if you are trying to go fast or race for long distances.

The fourth stroke is the *butterfly*, in which swimmers stay on their chests and move their arms in unison over the water—somewhat like the fluttering of a butterfly's wings—and then make a strong pull underneath the water. This stroke is accompanied by a "dolphin kick," in which the legs move up and down together in the water. The butterfly stroke, an innovation based on the breaststroke, is a thing of great beauty and power when it is done well, and for short distances it approaches the speed of the freestyle.

The following chart shows the relative speed of these four strokes and the current men's and women's 100-meter world record times for each.

Relative Speeds of Swimming Strokes
Current 100-Meter World Records

Stroke	Meters/Second	For Men	For Women
Freestyle (front crawl)	2.17	46.25 s	51.70 s
Butterfly	1.98	49.07 s	55.95 s
Backstroke	1.84	49.99 s	56.71 s
Breaststroke	1.67	57.47 s	63.86 s

Source: International Olympic Committee

What makes the breaststroke, the slowest of the competitive strokes, most interesting from our perspective is the fact that until 1873 it was the fastest way a white person had ever figured out how to swim competitively.

Different Strokes for Different Swimming Folks
We know that people have been swimming the breaststroke

since the Stone Age, according to pictures found in the Cave of Swimmers in southwestern Egypt, near the border with Libya. So the stroke has a rich and potentially 10,000-year-old history.

How these early people learned to swim the breast-stroke is not entirely clear, although it does have some resemblance to the way that some dogs, frogs, and many other animals swim.

We have the chance to discover information about practically everything that has occurred on our planet and beyond.

We also have reason to believe that native people in the Americas, the Pacific Islands, and parts of West Africa have been swimming the crawl—the faster way to swim—for several thousand years. Unfortunately, lacking a good Internet connection, direct flights, or the Discovery Channel, no one in Europe learned this until 1844, and then it was somewhat by accident. That was when a swimming competition was held in London, England, and two Native American swimmers actually showed up. Their unorthodox, or somewhat radical, stroke and its greater speed must have shocked the locals as they won several of the races—though apparently it did not shock them enough to change the way they swam. That would have to wait until 1873.

For the next twenty-nine years, Europeans continued to work to refine the breaststroke, making subtle but significant improvements to increase their speed and efficiency. The slowest swimmers continued to get faster at the slowest stroke, and they seemed content to do this. Yet halfway around the world, people native to other places swam much differently and much faster despite the fact that they were less consumed with the formal notion of swimming competitions and winning prizes.

Enter John Trudgen, the coach for a swim club in London. He was, by all accounts, a regular guy with a sense of curiosity and a keen desire to help his charges swim faster. No longer content with the limitations of the breaststroke, he would travel to South America in 1873 in search of new ideas about swimming. Based on observing native South American swimmers he developed his own version of the crawl. In Trudgen's version, a swimmer's arms recovered outside the water as his or her body rolled from side to side. This motion was coupled with a scissor kick with every two arm pulls. Trudgen taught this technique to the members of his club, and while the kick proved to be somewhat inefficient, it still produced much faster times than the breaststroke. Soon top English swimmers were swimming this crawl successfully in competition in addition to the breaststroke.

However, problems remained with the kick, and in 1902 Australian Richard Cavill discovered a missing piece of the puzzle by observing the swimming technique of people native to the Solomon Islands. Their version of the crawl combined an up-and-down, or "flutter," kick with the over-arm stroke. The result was a much smoother, more efficient, and faster way to swim. Cavill would teach this new method to his six sons, all of whom went on to become championship swimmers. Suddenly, in two relatively quick iterations, everyday genius had unlocked a better way to do something—not a new way

We too must figure out how to get our companies and organizations to deliver unique and compelling value if we intend to win.

that had never been done before but a way that was new and revolutionary for a group of people who took swimming very seriously. As a result, the world of competitive swimming would never be the same. After thousands of years, white people had finally figured out how to swim fast.

Today We Have No Good Excuses

In the 1840s people could be excused for not knowing everything. They could even be excused for their unwillingness to change in the face of better ideas about how to do things. After all, change is hard for people, even now in the twenty-first century—though one might wonder why it took them so long to change in the face of compelling evidence that there was a better way to swim.

This prompts some questions: Are we doing a host of other things as well as we could? Or have the limitations of our own knowledge or culture limited our ability to compete in life and our organizations' ability to compete in the marketplace? What if there are more brilliant ways to do things? And what if those more brilliant ways are all around us simply waiting for us to discover them? What if they are both obvious and less obvious, i.e., requiring us to scratch below the surface or to look at something with a slightly different eye?

In a sense John Trudgen's job was easy. He didn't have to scratch far beneath the surface to find people swimming in different and better ways. Yet he was the first person to take that insight and actually do something with it.

Today we can say, just a bit sarcastically, that we have the ability for the first time ever to know practically everything—or at least we have the chance to discover information about practically everything that has occurred on our planet and beyond. That doesn't mean we have figured out everything. But access to information is not our problem. The Internet, while lacking quality control, has suddenly put a world of possibilities at our fingertips. And travel, within reasonable time and cost, is now possible to virtually any place on the globe. So we don't have to wait for someone with a unique and better way of doing things to crash the party. We just need to know where and how to look for insight, or we just need to take a chance and look for insight that we can apply to the challenges and opportunities we face.

We don't have to be geniuses to make it happen. We just have to be someone who cares about swimming, or whatever we choose to excel at. Someone who is open to unlocking better ways. So if there is a poster child for this book, it is probably swim coach John Trudgen, a man who would have toiled in relative obscurity had he not possessed the curiosity of a child and the openness to try something new, qualities that moved him ahead of his contemporaries.

If we can't all figure out how to swim differently, we won't be in our pools for very long!

But what about us and the companies and organizations we live in? I will argue that we have no choice. So let's get out of the pool and be clear about the real challenge we face. If we can't all figure out how to swim differently, we won't be in our pools for very long! Just as Trudgen sought to figure out how to get his swimmers to win races, we too must figure out how to get our companies and organizations to deliver unique and compelling value if we intend to win.

Unless your customers are enamored with the breaststroke, you'd better find a new way to swim.

Chapter Two

The Quest for Compelling Value

Or ...
Why you have to reinvent the game if you hope to win.

What do a car rental company that picks you up, an electronic device that allows you to create your own customized entertainment experience, and the world's largest chain of natural food supermarkets have in common? If we are creative, we might suggest that taken together they attend to the most essential needs of human beings in our fast-paced world: mobility, amusement, and nourishment. But as you and I know, there is a lot more to life than that.

In the simplest business terms, Enterprise Rent-a-Car, the Apple iPod, and Whole Foods Market are joined by the fact that each changed the way things were done in very crowded marketplaces by providing new and compelling value for the customers they chose to serve. They did it in an almost ninety-year-old service industry, in a fast-paced, high-technology world, and in the most basic business of selling food (a business that one might argue is really the world's oldest profession). Their stories provide a helpful reference point for understanding what all of our companies and organizations need to do to create customer and business success.

A Pickup Line That Mattered

To understand the compelling value of Enterprise Rent-a-Car, let's quickly step back in time to the history of the car rental business. Hertz was the pioneer in car rental and traces its origins to 1918 when Walter Jacobs, age twenty-two, opened a car rental business in Chicago with a fleet of twelve Model T Fords. Something tells me that renting Model Ts today would also be a hit, but let's not race ahead of ourselves. Five years later Jacobs sold his growing concern to John Hertz, president of the Yellow Cab and Yellow Truck and Coach Manufacturing Company, and the Hertz "Drive-Ur-Self System" would be born.

As the creator of an emerging industry, Hertz was an amazing innovator. The company launched a series of firsts that would keep it at the forefront of the car rental business. These innovations included the first coast-to-coast car rental network (1925), the first car rental credit card (1926), the first airport location at Midway Airport in Chicago (1932), the first program that allowed renters to drop off their cars at a different location (1933), the first centralized billing system (1959), the first frequent travelers club (1972), and the first computerized driving instructions (1984). This constant commitment to delivering value in what we might call the conventional car rental business kept the company in the lead.

In fact, Hertz's most formidable competitor for many years was Avis—the company that seemed to cherish the underdog role and gained attention with a popular ad campaign that stated "We're No. 2 but we try harder." And Avis did try very hard. Founded in 1946 by Warren Avis at Willow Run Airport in Detroit, the company quickly expanded across the United States and then into Europe, Canada, and Mexico. It followed Hertz's airport-centric business model based on growing recognition that airlines were becoming the dominant mode of long-distance travel. As a worthy competitor, Avis introduced its share of innovations, including the first real-time reservation and information management system (1972), the first automated self-serve check-in service (1984), the first handheld computer for processing a car return in the return lot (1987), and the first handheld GPS system (2003). Until recently, Avis's hard work enabled the company to remain No. 2. But even though the innovations did enhance customer value, they did not change the game.

So where does Enterprise fit into the picture? Its story begins in 1957 when a young man named Jack Taylor decided to test the emerging idea of leasing cars in St. Louis. While auto leasing was not a bad idea, his best idea came when customers suggested that he rent cars to them while their own cars were in the shop for repairs. So with an initial fleet of seventeen vehicles he began to rent "loaners" for $6 a day and 6 cents a mile.

Unlike Hertz and Avis, Taylor believed that the best opportunities to grow his company were with "hometown renters" and not travelers arriving at airports. These

But even though Avis's innovations did enhance customer value, they did not change the game.

were people whose cars were in the shop for maintenance or because of an accident. This different focus led to opening branches where people lived and worked rather than on the grounds of airports. Also unlike Hertz and Avis, the evolution of Enterprise was not characterized by a stream of innovations in technology and the customer interface. Other than its clear and unique market focus and its commitment to being as close to its target customers as possible, the company's biggest innovation was probably an amazingly simple and compelling idea suggested by an everyday genius. In 1974 a branch manager in Orlando began to offer customers free rides to the rental office. This service became the "We'll Pick You Up" theme that is now an Enterprise tradition.

After establishing its new game and dominating its market, in 1995 the company began to compete head-on with the traditional car rental companies by opening its first airport location at Denver International Airport. Today Enterprise is the largest car rental company in North America and has almost 7,000 locations in the United States, Canada, United Kingdom, Ireland, and Germany. It also boasts having a location within 15 miles of 90 percent of the U.S. population. Hertz is still the largest car rental company in the world, but Avis is no longer No. 2. It remains a solid company with a loyal following but is now No. 4 or No. 5. The success of Enterprise Rent-a-Car is really a story about seeing an opportunity to refine a marketplace and deliver new and compelling value. But what about combining new technology with a dramatically different customer experience?

Going beyond the Latest Technology

To understand the compelling value proposition of the iPod, let's look at the genius of Sony, the first people to make music and entertainment personal and wearable. In 1979, this remarkably innovative Japanese company reinvented the world of personal entertainment with the introduction of the Walkman, a portable cassette tape player that could be taken anywhere. (I can hear some of you asking what a cassette tape player is, or as our teenage daughter Sara often remarks, "That's so last century!") The Walkman was truly a great liberator of people and music.

Before its invention you had to be at home near your stereo system or in your car to enjoy your favorite tunes. But Sony saw the opportunity to change the game: portable and wearable music that by using headphones you could take anywhere and listen to anytime. Its success was phenomenal. By its twentieth anniversary in 1999, Sony had sold 186 million cassette-tape Walkman units, 46 million CD Walkman units, 4.6 million mini-disc Walkman units, and more than 500 million sets of headphones. Sales increased every year for twenty straight years.

So it was a bit surprising when the people who owned the ears of a gigantic market lost their groove or at least failed to realize that it was time for the game they had changed to change again. The change would involve a new technology and an experience that could deliver far more compelling value for a new generation of music listeners. At about the time that Sony's Walkman was reaching its peak, the digital audio player—or MP3—was emerging and with it the potential to have and personalize an unlimited amount of music and entertainment.

The change would involve a new technology and an experience that could deliver far more compelling value for a new generation of music listeners.

Digital audio players, unlike the Walkman, were devices that could store, organize, and play digital music files. In fact, the first mass-marketed player, the Rio PMP300 from Diamond Multimedia, was introduced in September 1998, and a flurry of activity began as established companies and entrepreneurial start-ups raced to create a winning product. But it was Apple Computer that would, at least for now, become the big winner—not by having the perfect product, although the iPod is very impressive, but by having the most compelling customer experience. This combination of the iPod itself, iTunes software, and the iTunes store delivers compelling customer value. With the iPod's combination of brilliant design, small size, and ease of use and iTunes' access to the most songs, Apple was positioned perfectly. With its clever marketing and advertising and a major investment in refinement, upgrading, and versatility—including the ability to watch videos and other programming—iPod quickly became one of the hottest products on the planet. By the end of 2006, more than 67 million iPods had been sold and more than 2 billion iTunes songs had been downloaded.

The proof is in the experience. When you buy an iPod and log on to the iTunes Web site, your notion of personal entertainment and its possibilities will be transformed. This is not to say that Apple's market dominance is ensured. At the time of this writing several other leading companies, including Microsoft, are making major investments to compete. The wild card here could be cell phone providers like Verizon, Sprint, and Cingular, who, along with their equipment partners, are producing a new generation of cell phones with built-in MP3 players. This fusion of technologies could again quickly change the game. In the fast-paced, high-stakes world of electronic technology, the challenge to deliver new and more compelling value is even greater. But what about something as basic as the retail grocery business?

Selling a Way of Life and a Set of Values

To understand the compelling-value proposition of Whole Foods Markets, we should probably look back in time to the beginning of the human experience, when people ate natural food out of necessity if and when they could either catch it or grow it. But in the late 1970s the world of natural and organic food appealed only to a relatively small segment of the market. Stores were stocked with a limited array of natural products that included organic produce and dairy products, beans, grains, vegetarian cuisine, vitamins and herbal supplements, and healthy baked goods that often lacked taste, texture, and general appeal. These places appealed to a market niche that was disproportionately populated by people who wore Birkenstocks and lived in college towns, and they seemed to turn off mainstream food buyers.

Yet how many people would be interested in eating healthier and safer foods if

The proof is in the experience.

they thought that the choices and the environment were more amenable to shoppers' habits and tastes? That's where, in 1980, four natural-food entrepreneurs in Austin, Texas, saw an opportunity to change the game by making the connection with the supermarket, an environment that had come to dominate grocery shopping. Today, with sales of roughly $5 billion, Whole Foods Market is the world's leading retailer of natural and organic foods, operating stores in North America and the United Kingdom.

Visit a Whole Foods Market and you are likely to rethink your notion of healthy food. Enter through the produce department with its exquisite bounty of some of nature's most beautiful creations in all their radiant colors and shapes. Pass the fresh fish counter, the meat counter filled with hormone-free and naturally raised beef, and the gourmet prepared foods section and taste samples along the way. Look at the offerings in the bakery, which say everything about delicious and very little about the crunchy granola that one associates with natural foods. Then find the more traditional natural food offerings that are full of life, energy, and dramatically attractive packaging, in part because the world of healthy eating has exploded along with the growth of Whole Foods. This is the bold new world of natural and organic foods, not the crunchy, low- or no-fat, fiber-filled world of the recent past, although a lot of those things can be found, too.

Equally important to Whole Foods' value proposition is the company's commitment to educate customers about healthy eating and healthy lifestyles through written materials, demonstrations in the stores, cooking classes, community involvement, and support for the issues of health and building and maintaining a healthy food supply.

There are more remarkable stores in some respects. Wegman's and its amazing food emporiums come to mind. But Whole Foods is selling a concept—about food, ourselves, the communities we live in, and the planet we share—that is compelling for a growing number of people, even with its high prices relative to many traditional supermarkets. And now a new set of competitors—companies like Trader Joe's and even Wal-Mart— is challenging this formula and pushing to make natural and organic food a lower-cost commodity. It will be interesting to see how Whole Foods evolves as it works to defend the industry and values it created. Delivering and maintaining compelling value is a never-ending process.

You Win by Changing the Game

Many other companies and organizations have changed the game in a way that matters to the customers they serve. In fact, it would be fun and useful for you to come up with your own short list, but don't stop with companies and organizations. Think of people from other walks of life who succeeded in a big way by being different.

If you're stuck, think about someone like the King of Rock 'n' Roll—Elvis Presley. He probably didn't start out or end life as a genius. He probably didn't begin to sing with a plan to transform the music business. But along the road between Tupelo, Mississippi, and Memphis, Tennessee, he found the song within himself. The song was based on an inspiring combination of the gospel music he heard in Southern churches and Memphis's all-night gospel sings, the rhythm and blues (R&B) that filled the Mecca that is Beale Street, the country music of the South, and the popular music of his time. Elvis combined these into his own sound, and aided by his own sensuality, charm, and humor he created a unique and compelling customer experience.

In the fast-paced, high-stakes world of electronic technology, the challenge to deliver new and more compelling value is even greater.

Or think about the amazing James Brown, a singer and performer affectionately known as "The Godfather of Soul" and "The Hardest Working Man in Show Business." In a career that spanned six decades, his innovations in rhythm and the very nature of his musical performance changed the course of R&B and soul music, profoundly influenced rock and roll, and eventually inspired today's rap artists. He also revolutionized how people danced, crossing over racial groups and social classes.

As you are probably realizing, changing the game means looking around you at the world of customers specifically and at the world itself in general.

Were the people behind these ideas brilliant, and were their ideas brilliant? In a sense the answer to both questions is "yes." After all, each saw a market opportunity that others had not yet seen. And in doing so, each presented the market with a fresh and new value proposition. Renting a car was not a new idea. Neither was the digital music player. And people have been eating natural and organic food for most of human history. In fact, relatively recent development of chemical preservatives and unnatural ingredients is the only reason we are no longer eating natural food. Elvis and James Brown didn't create new forms of music from scratch. They were standing on the shoulders of some amazing people who were standing on the shoulders of their amazing ancestors and adapting their music to the environments, circumstances, and geographies (broadly defined) that they found themselves in. So the real genius in each was an ability to see things differently than others and to put things together in a different way. We can all be like them with a spark of inspiration tied to a challenge or opportunity that confronts us, our customers, and our companies or organizations.

Focusing on customer success is the key to business and organizational success. We need to change the game in order to win. In changing the game we need to seek fresh ideas.

This was made crystal clear to me in another moment of great honesty that almost cost me a very interesting assignment. A number of years ago I was invited to make a presentation about differentiation and delivering compelling customer value to the leadership team of a major regional bank. The bank was the largest in its market but doing very poorly in terms of customer service. I arrived at the meeting with a few ideas, a lot of questions, and, I hoped, an open mind.

Visit a Whole Foods Market and you are likely to rethink your notion of healthy food.

After we exchanged greetings, I said that I was excited to meet them as I had reviewed material on their company and was impressed with its rich history and sustained growth. The bank was clearly a major player in its region, although in the past few years it had been losing key customers to competitors who offered a higher level of service. They replied that they were excited to talk with me as well. Although they had already met with a couple of large consulting firms, the CEO had been told by a peer that I might have a refreshing perspective on their challenge. I expressed my appreciation. Then one of the executives handed me a copy of a study they had recently commissioned on the customer service practices of the leading banks in the country and the following conversation ensued:

> Executive: "We've done some very important work in anticipation of meeting with you and the other consultants. Here's a detailed study that we just commissioned."
>
> Me: "Very interesting." I briefly skimmed the table of contents and the summary of ideas and recommendation. "Or should I say very amusing."

With that I began to laugh, not a huge laugh but a laugh nonetheless.

> Executive: "You're laughing because this is good, right?"
>
> Me: "Actually, I'm laughing because it is funny. I typically laugh when things are funny and often when things are good and funny. But this is, from my limited perspective, just plain funny!"

Probably not the best way to start a meeting like this.

> Executive: "The other firms we talked with seemed impressed. In what sense do you think that it is funny?"
>
> Me: "Well, at the risk of being viewed as inappropriate, can I ask all of you a simple question?"

Executive: "Certainly."

Me: "Are banks renowned for providing the highest level of customer service?"

Executive: "Probably not."

Me: "Then that is what's funny. You have, with all due respect, spent over a million dollars to study the customer service practices of companies that are not very good at customer service. It's kind of like my spending money to study the consulting skills of kangaroos."

Executive: "Well, what should we have done?"

Me: "Study the best companies and organizations in industries that are renowned for providing the highest level of customer service to the most demanding customers."

Executive: "That makes sense."

Me: "I agree. It's not funny. But it makes sense. If you really want to be great at customer service, you need to create a new and better commitment to the customer."

And strangely enough they hired me to lead them on a journey to figure out what they could learn from the world's leading providers of customer service—companies like Nordstrom's, Ritz-Carlton, and USAA Insurance and organizations like AARP.

I'd like to say that there was a happy ending to this story at least as far as the bank was concerned. The team that was assigned to the project was talented and thoughtful, and its members worked hard to figure out how to reinvent customer service in the banking industry. But their boldest proposals were rejected by senior leadership and the board as too radical for their 150-year-old institution and ended up being taken by some of the participants to more innovative financial institutions that would change the game. Their bank would continue to struggle with customer service and eventually be bought for its market share by a more innovative competitor.

This story is not uncommon. Too many companies have trouble getting out of the trap they are in because they are unwilling to think strategically about how to change their game. Instead they talk about near-term profitability, EBITDA, short-term revenues, their stock price, earnings per share, shareholder value, and the like as though these things are the essence of strategic thinking rather than measures of whether the organization is truly meeting the evolving needs of its customers. For these companies, customer success is too difficult to measure every quarter.

You Win by Making Customers Successful

So what does it take to make our customers successful? It all depends on what they are trying to accomplish, because their purpose rather than ours should guide our strategy, our commitment to innovation, and the products, services, and solutions we offer. Peter Drucker, whose core ideas will always be relevant to business thinking, said many years ago that there were three fundamental questions every company (and every organization) should ask:

- "Who are our customers?"
- "What are their needs?"
- "What do they consider value?"

Drucker understood that customers, their evolving needs, and their evolving perception of value should drive any business or organization. If we can move forward with them, we can remain relevant. If we focus on short-term financial measures,

we run the risk of missing the mark. So we probably need to add
the following three questions to make things perfectly clear:

- How are customers' needs and considerations of value
  changing?
- Where do they see their world going?
- Where could we imagine their world going?

Thinking about these questions gives us a lot of options for
changing the game in our business. For example, we can deliver:

- The most uniquely valuable products, services, and solu-
  tions
- A whole new level of quality and performance
- Different and better technology
- A quantum leap in responsiveness and or speed
- Knowledge that makes the customer smarter and more
  powerful
- Vision to get them to the future

If customers' needs and what they consider to be value
remained static, we probably would not have to change very
much or very quickly. Pick a winning formula, work out the
details, and keep delivering it with skill. But customer needs
change whether they are consumers, citizens, businesses, governments, or organizations. Their lives or worlds become more
complicated or faster paced; they have less time or fewer
resources with which to get more done; they decide to focus on
their core activities; they get smarter; they have more options;
they ask more questions; they need more guidance; they worry
about the details; they face critical challenges and opportunities;
they revolt from being treated poorly; and they see the potential
of technology to improve the way they live, work, or play or
they decide to do business with fewer vendors.

Sometimes the changes are hard to figure out. But often they are obvious to those willing to pay attention. Were Honda and Toyota the only car companies that knew there was a finite supply of petroleum in the earth and that gas prices were likely to increase significantly over time? We didn't need a few million dollars' worth of market research to figure that one out. But surprisingly, they were the only two cars companies that had a sense of urgency about the evolving world of their customers.

Sometimes the changes are a result of major demographic shifts as new generations bring their own ways of doing things. Take Generation Y's approach to buying a car and the success of the Scion car brand. In studying this market segment, Toyota understood that Gen Y didn't want the same car or the same car-buying experience as their parents. So the company decided to change the product game and the entire customer experience. It created cars that were affordable and hip but had only a limited number of colors and options to choose from. One of those options was a snowboard rack. Toyota coupled this with set prices and the ability to buy the cars online without having to deal with a pushy salesperson. None of

Delivering and maintaining compelling value is a never-ending process.

the specific parts were unique, but the entire offering represented a new game, one that has been so successful in its first few years that Toyota is in the enviable position of being able to control the quantity of Scions it produces.

Sometimes customers recognize that they have a right to demand greater value even when there are a limited number of suppliers. Take the example of students applying for assistance under the Federal government's student loan program. Until recently students could wait several weeks for a response to a loan application. Under the new game, applicants can receive preliminary approval of their loans within a matter of moments using roughly the same business model and technology that private-sector credit card companies use. This commitment to understanding the challenge that students face as they try to make such an important life decision is one of the best stories in a new era of public sector responsiveness to the citizens (i.e., customers) it serves. The emerging trend across agencies at all levels of government is encouraging, but it requires a real strategic sense of what it means to deliver compelling value.

And You Win by Delivering Compelling Value

Compelling value means changing in a major way the customer experience or the results the customer gets from the experience. It is not about making an incremental difference. The time for that has passed.

Talk is cheap. If we really want to stand out from the pack, we need to act in ways that generate real value for customers. The good news is that in most industries it isn't that hard to stand out from the pack. Not that most companies aren't working overtime to make it sound as though they offer unique value. Simply check the marketing materials, Web sites, and advertisements of companies in your industry or any industry with which you are familiar, and you are likely to be bombarded with glowing self-praise.

Even companies that have a track record of less than stellar performance are claiming to be "driven by innovation," "obsessed with quality," committed to "going the extra mile to serve our customers," staffed with the "most highly trained and dedicated people," "recognized by organizations like J.D. Power and Associates," supported by "world class systems and processes," and "offering the finest guarantee available." It is enough to make a grown person cry. Remember how Ford Motor Company was constantly telling the world that "Quality Is Job One!" while it consistently lagged behind its competitors in product quality. Maybe they were simply stating their objective, but the implication was that they were great at product quality.

So even if your company hasn't been brilliant in the past, now is your chance to shine. All you need is a real market opportunity, a commitment to understand the customers in that market

So the real genius in each was an ability to see things differently than others and to put things together in a different way.

better than anyone else, a willingness to think about where the market and the customers' needs are going or could be going in the future, and a commitment to identify and deliver compelling value.

And you need to agree to abide by six basic rules:

First, you can't win unless you are really different in a way that really matters to the customers you choose to serve.

Second, you can't be really different in ways that matter unless you understand the customers better than anyone else and can craft the best solution to meet their real needs.

Third, you can't win unless you commit to delivering value throughout the entire customer experience from start to finish.

Fourth, you can't win unless you have a clear focus or framework for delivering value.

Fifth, you can't win unless whatever you're offering provides the right combination of tangible and intangible value. Even the best products must be surrounded by the best customer experience. And even the best customer experiences must be wrapped around a product, service, or solution that is itself valuable to the customer.

Sixth, you can't win unless everyone in your organization believes passionately in the value of what you offer and is given the tools and support to deliver their part of it with passion and skill.

Seventh, you can't win unless you are committed to continually raising the bar.

A Framework for Delivering Compelling Value

1. Be different in a way that really matters to the customers you choose to serve.
2. Understand the customer better than anyone else and craft the best solution.
3. Deliver real value throughout the entire customer experience.
4. Deliver value based on a clear and consistent focus or framework.
5. Deliver the right combination of tangible and intangible value.
6. Build an organization that is passionate about the value you offer and gives people the tools and support to make a difference.
7. Commit to continually raising the bar.

Now let's turn our attention to why companies and organizations and the geniuses in them have so much trouble coming up with the right ideas.

chapter Three

Genius in Chains

Or . . .

Why traditional approaches to strategy, innovation, and marketing no longer make any sense, and what to do about it.

I f challenges and opportunities abound, why do most people and organizations have so much trouble unlocking the genius in themselves? Maybe they are going about it in the wrong way.

Picture this scene that takes place almost every day in companies and organizations around the globe as groups meet to attack a pressing business problem or unlock an amazing new opportunity.

They gather in conference rooms, board rooms, lunch rooms, corner offices, hallways lined with pictures of past successes, private rooms at local restaurants, conference or retreat centers, or sometimes outside, if the weather permits. They are armed with flip charts, brightly colored markers, Post-it Notes®, spreadsheets, PowerPoint presentations, market studies, customer surveys, competitive intelligence, boatloads of information downloaded from the Internet, props and toys, a trained or untrained facilitator, a sense of urgency, and a list of

questions possibly inspired by Socrates. Each element is intended to spark their creativity, get them "out of the box"—free from
the powerful grip of everyday thinking (and their current reality)—and lead to a breakthrough that will at least ensure their
organization's survival and at best revolutionize their world and
life as we and, hopefully, the customers know it.

**It's hard to be brilliant
sitting on our butts.**

At the epic moment
when the late arrivals have
finally appeared, received kid-
ding and absolution for their
tardiness, secured the essential super-sized mug of caffeine, and
taken their seats, the leader of the session begins. "We are at a critical point," he or she laments in a tone reminiscent of some classic
movies, "when the future of our group, product, service, organization, entire civilization, or _____ (fill in the blank)
hangs in the balance. The clock is ticking," he or she continues.
"Our backs are to the wall, and we must come up with a newer,
better, faster, stronger, easier, or otherwise more innovative
approach"—i.e., we must build a better mousetrap and a better
mouse. Then after a dramatic pause, he or she utters the dreaded
and overused phrase: "So who has an out-of-the-box idea?!"

Now there's a moment of silence, possibly to pay tribute to
those who have tried before them. However, more likely it's
because everyone in the room has wrestled unsuccessfully with
this issue before, has no idea why they were chosen for this
assignment, is less than eager to put the first marginal idea on
the table, or is just plain clueless about what to do. And even
though they are told that "there is no such thing as a bad idea,"
those with ideas fear the silent scorn and cleverly crafted smirks
that might accompany the floating of some half-baked thought.
Amid the crash of pins dropping, the subtle sound of sarcasm
quickly begins to fill the room.

"Ohhh?!? You want out-of-the-box ideas!" is the quiet yet resounding cry of those who, in an earlier life, would have been the first to step out on a limb or swing from the monkey bars without a net or a parent to catch them. Then after a moment of silent meditation, a spokesperson for the creatively challenged summons the courage to speak:

"Are we talking about totally new ideas here? I mean things we've never thought of before? Or are we just supposed to come up with a better way of doing what we're already doing?" In other words, should we dust off the same old tired ideas that we've always had for solving this problem and hope that the customer thinks it's at least a semi-quantum leap forward?

"Some new ideas would be great," encourages the group's leader. "After all, the world and our market are changing faster than we ever imagined." This means one of the following: "Competitor X has just launched its amazing new self-fixing gizmo"; or "Competitor Y has just unveiled its new proactive service warranty"; or "Competitor Z has just dropped prices 25 percent in an insane (and possibly quite effective) move to crush us like a bug"; or "The citizens we serve are about to revolt if we don't figure out how to dramatically reduce response time."

Now the cat—cleverly disguised as a culture of plodding incrementalism—is out of the bag. A scary picture in any world, let alone one that requires dramatic change and fresh thinking.

Breakthroughs occur when we engage the world with our senses turned on full blast and with a readiness to notice and question everything.

"So we need really new ideas," he or she continues. "Breakthrough ideas. Ideas that will shake up the way we do our business. And they need to be implementable by the start of next quarter or before the next total eclipse of our bottom-line—whichever comes first."

And then he or she scans the room in the hope that some-one, inspired by the moment, will say, "In that case I have a head full of new, creative, and totally brilliant ideas to put on the table." But it is not to be.

Like Benjamin Franklin, we have to stand in a storm to be truly inspired (or electrified).

So, lacking a better alternative, they do what any group of self-respecting adults would do. They roll up their sleeves, grab their coffee or soda, and get start-ed. Everyone tries to brain-storm as hard as possible, which is no small feat given the big constraints of their collective years of formal education combined with the time they've spent in this or any other similar organization (that has been systematically sucking the creativity out of them since the day they arrived).

For a brief moment at the outset, there is some hope that the stars will align and the gods, or at least the Tooth Fairy, will bring forth from their collective knowledge, wisdom, and expe-rience at least one great and novel idea that will light up the white board, gather momentum, and move into the marketplace (after overcoming a host of internal barriers along the way). But beyond the retreaded concepts and modest enhancements to existing efforts, magic rarely ever springs forth from the confines of their home for the day.

Few breakthroughs happen this way. It's hard to be brilliant sitting on our butts.

Breakthroughs Require Engagement and Imagination

Breakthroughs occur when we engage the world with our senses turned on full blast and with a readiness to notice and question everything. They occur when we bring new stuff into our world and test the bounds of other people's best thinking against the needs of our customers and our industry. They occur when smart and engaged people are challenged to rediscover the wonder and curiosity of their childhood in a focused and passionate way—by wandering aimfully beyond the boundaries of what we are already comfortable knowing. Barring this, our best intentions are doomed to fail.

Breakthroughs Occur When We Engage and Imagine.

They build on something that already exists. Even the most brilliant ideas have always been inspired by something that someone else has done, thought or dreamed . . . in another company or organization, another country or culture, another walk of life, or a walk in the woods, or the jungle, or along the shore. Birds inspired planes; gospel music inspired rock and roll; a boot maker with small-town values inspired thinking about customer satisfaction; the idea of eliminating the middleman inspired one of the world's largest personal computer makers; the healing power of plants has inspired many successful medicines; and so on. It is this inspiration that can rarely be reproduced by simply convening and "brainstorming." Like Benjamin Franklin, we have to stand in a storm to be

This sense of vision— of seeing new and better possibilities—is what makes truly great companies, organizations, and people stand out from the pack.

truly inspired (or electrified) by it. And when we do that, something starts to click.

Business and organizational success is all about being different in ways that deliver greater value to our customers. But we can do things differently only if we see things differently. This sense of vision—of seeing new and better possibilities—is what makes truly great companies, organizations, and people stand out from the pack. Being different doesn't mean that we have to create brilliant and valuable ideas from scratch, although that would certainly be nice. We can win by unlocking the possibilities in someone else's great ideas and being the first (or the best) at adapting them to our industry or marketplace. Our real task is to find the right ideas.

The only skills you will need are an understanding of what is important to your customers, an open mind, and a sense of curiosity.

This book will show you how to transform your company, organization, agency, or nonprofit association by using the best thinking the world has to offer. It is a challenge to change the way you think about success and innovation, from the nearly impossible task of discovering a one-of-a-kind breakthrough to the very possible task of uncovering the potential of an already-tested idea and applying it to your circumstances. The only skills you will need are an understanding of what is important to your customers, an open mind, and a sense of curiosity.

chapter Four

Curiosity as Competitive Advantage

Or . . .
Why our innate gift for curiosity is the only real weapon in the battle to remain relevant and how to rediscover it and...

Why geography matters and why a thirteenth-century traveler might be the most important business thinker of the twenty-first-century....

Have you ever wondered what Velcro, barbed wire, and chainsaws have in common? If you thought they could all be purchased at a hardware store, you'd be right. If you thought all three were useful inventions, you'd be right as well. And if you thought they could all be used as props in a scary movie, you'd probably be right again. But if you imagined for a moment that their inventors were pretty clever people, you'd be only partly right. Their real brilliance, it turns out, was a willingness to take a "field trip" into the world around them, equipped simply with a sense of curiosity and an ability to see things in a very different way.

It's 1948, and Georges de Mestral, a Swiss engineer and avid hiker, is taking a walk in the woods with his dog. As he looks down, he notices that his socks and his dog are covered with burrs. Had he been like the rest of us, he might have just pulled them off and thrown them away. After all, we can only assume that burrs have been clinging to people and animals for a long time. But in his mind there was something remarkable about a small piece of nature that could instantly attach itself to creatures passing by and stick so well that it was hard to remove. So he took some burrs home to study under a microscope. What he discovered was a surface of tiny hooks that locked themselves to practically any fuzzy thing. It was a discovery that would lead him to conceive of Velcro, a product with literally thousands of uses today.

Barbed wire, chainsaws, and countless other inventions have similar stories. Barbed wire was invented in 1868 by a gentleman named Michael Kelly, who observed that thorny hedges were an effective way to keep livestock contained. His original patent was almost identical in its design to the branches of the plants he observed. The chainsaw was invented in 1946 by a fellow named Joseph Cox who based his design on the amazing cutting ability of wood-eating insects. His resulting chain with cutters recreated the action of the timber beetle's mandible (lower jawbone) as it worked its way through a tree.

Today, even the most creative and successful ideas have their roots planted firmly in the work of others.

Those are just a few relatively recent examples. Remember Icarus's early attempt to copy birds? Little did he know that it would take a few thousand additional years of field trips, study, and design to get it right (or Wright, to salute those inventive brothers from Ohio). Today, even the most creative and successful ideas have their roots planted firmly in the work of others. Try to imagine the amazing creations of Pixar Animation Studios without the magic of the original Walt Disney Studios, or the simple genius of eBay without any understanding of the evolution of auctions—a phenomenon that dates back to 500 B.C. and was first described by Herodotus—or the prevalence of pizza delivery without realizing that more than a century ago horse-drawn carriages brought milk to most people's doors.

> **What would happen if each of us looked for insight and inspiration in the world around us and then applied it in some practical or powerful way?**

Were these people and others like them much smarter than you, me, our coworkers, and the rest of the Dilberts with whom we share our little planet? Or could we, under the right circumstances, be equally brilliant? What would happen if each of us looked for insight and inspiration in the world around us and then applied it in some practical or powerful way? The answer might surprise you. But you'll have to stick with me, kind of like Velcro, in order to figure it out.

Curiosity Is the Essential Starting Point

Remember *Jack and the Beanstalk*? In this classic children's story, Jack makes a decision that will change his family's life forever. He and his mother are running out of food, and she asks him to sell the family's only cow at the marketplace, presumably for the highest price. Along the way Jack meets a strange-looking man who offers him five magic seeds in exchange for the cow, promising him, "If you plant them overnight, by morning they will grow right up to the sky." For a hungry young boy living from meal to meal, the offer seems too good to pass up. The man, well-versed in sales skills and with an ability to quickly assess the potential customer's predicament, even offers a give-your-cow-back guarantee if the seeds do not perform as promised. With little hesitation, Jack agrees to the deal and heads home to tell his mother about their good fortune.

What if we pursue the road less taken to an uncertain destination?

Needless to say, she is far from impressed. In fact, she is convinced that their sorry state is about to get even worse and her only child is the biggest fool in the parish. In anger she throws the seeds out the window. In her eyes Jack has screwed up big time. In his eyes there is something intriguing about the possibility of seeds that will grow to the sky, even if there is no assurance that they will lead him to great wealth.

The next morning, as promised, a beanstalk has grown up to the sky, and Jack eagerly decides to climb it. Emerging from a cloud, he arrives at a long road that leads to a big house belonging to a giant ogre and his oversized wife. The ogre—who delights in eating children—has a lot of gold, and Jack takes one of the bags of gold and escapes down the beanstalk before he becomes dinner.

But Jack is not content, and we are led to believe that his curiosity gets the better of him. He makes two more trips up the beanstalk and back to the big house, first to take the goose that lays the golden eggs and then to take the golden harp—again eluding the ogre as he races back down the beanstalk. By most versions of the story, Jack and his mother then become rich and live happily ever after. As for the ogre, there is no apparent reason to be sad. After all, it wasn't until the creation of *Shrek* that anyone saw the possibility of an ogre being a hero.

We need to be a bit more like Jack, not necessarily choosing to exchange something of value for magic seeds or stealing something that doesn't belong to us, but in wondering what would happen if we head up a beanstalk on a journey to unlock greater value for our customers. What if we pursue the road less taken to an uncertain destination? Selling the family's cow for a limited amount of money would have simply prolonged his family's sad state of affairs. Jack needed to change the game, and the seeds were his only apparent ticket.

Where should the rest of us look for magic seeds?

On a focused journey to the world that is beyond our current comfort zone.

Beyond the Flat World

In his book *The World Is Flat,* Thomas Friedman makes the case for a new economic world order that seems to have emerged almost overnight. He identifies the hallmarks of this world as the new Internet-based digital economy and the phenomenon of outsourcing in which a significant share of U.S. economic activity and support services (and presumably those of other developed countries) can be done anywhere in the world where the cost is lower and the quality is reasonable. A good example of this is the emergence of Bangalore in India as the IT support hub for a growing universe of companies and industries, though the results of this shift are still uneven for many customers.

Friedman contends that in this new world order anyone has the chance to win. But what does his assessment

Deliver compelling value or perish.

mean for us as individuals and companies whose livelihoods could quickly disappear over fiber-optic lines? Deliver compelling value or perish, I presume.

But the world is even flatter than Friedman and other leading thinkers realize. Although it would be ideal to travel the world in search of markets, suppliers, and outsourcing centers, its real potential is the variety of ideas, insights, and ways of doing things that are now readily accessible to all of us. We are only a few mouse clicks away from a wealth of information about practically anything that is going on or has gone on in the past. We are only a few more clicks away from some of the best thinking about what might go on in the future. So geography and all its wonder and diversity are now almost in the palms of our hands—or more aptly at the tips of our fingers—and this is cause for celebration.

To understand its potential in the twenty-first century, the best place to turn is to a family of traders and explorers from the thirteenth century, who demonstrated the power of looking for opportunities in a rich world around them. The most famous member of this family was Marco Polo, known for his travels to China and for his keen eye for the new ideas and ways of doing things that he found there and along the way.

We are only a few mouse clicks away from a wealth of information about practically anything that is going on or has gone on in the past.

Marco was born into an illustrious family of merchants who hailed from Venice, quite possibly the most important trading center in Europe at the time. His father and uncle had excelled as traders by continually seeking new business opportunities and stretching the bounds of their own known world. In 1271, at age seventeen, Marco joined them as they set out on their most ambitious journey. After sailing to the eastern edge of the Mediterranean Sea, they set out along the southern branch of the Silk Road, heading to China through Khotan, and then to the court of Kublai Khan, the grandson of Genghis Khan. It would take them three years to reach the court, in what is today Beijing.

The Silk Road had seen countless traders for many centuries. In Roman times, caravans headed to China carrying gold and other precious metals, as well as precious stones, ivory, and glass. Going the other direction were furs, ceramics, jade, bronze, iron, and exotic plants and animals never before seen in the west. But silk was thought by many westerners to be the most exotic discovery that came from Asia. Silk was not easy to make, and the Romans who first encountered it were told that it was made by a mysterious tribe in the east.

As important as all of these commodities were, the most important goods that came along the Silk Road were probably ideas about math, science, business, medicine, the workings of societies and governments, and even religion. We tend to think of Buddhism as an east Asian religion, but in fact it was brought to China from India along the Silk Road. Christianity also traveled along the Silk Road in the sixth and seventh centuries A.D. There is even reason to believe that Judaism found its way to China along the very same route.

The Polos were not the first Europeans of their generation to journey to China, and many skeptics questioned whether they got there at all. But upon his return to Venice, Marco Polo wrote a book about his roughly 20-year stay, called simply *The Travels of Marco Polo,* which was the first written document about China to appear in Europe. The book described a world so far beyond most people's grasp that they found it hard to believe (not unlike many Europeans in the nineteenth century who found it hard to believe that there was a faster

A new era of curiosity as the driver of economic activity had begun.

way to swim). But Marco Polo's book inspired some people to learn more about China and its people, geography, culture, customs, products, and inventions. It inspired others to seek their own fortune and fame. A new era of curiosity as the driver of economic activity had begun.

Today there is some question about whether Marco Polo's writings were based on his own observations or on stories he was told by others venturing along his route. In either case, his keen sense of curiosity and eye for detail were his greatest gifts. He was, more than 700 years ago, a great role model for all of us and for our companies and organizations. The challenge is to figure out in our own journeys what is worthy of our curiosity and attention. John Trudgen was focused on swimming, and his curiosity changed the course of swimming history. We need to be focused on our customers and markets to change the course of their history.

Now It's Time to Take Your Own Journeys

In the following chapters, I'm going to test your curiosity by taking you out of your day-to-day world on ten journeys to the future of customer and business success. We will go to some very different and quite remarkable places in search of insight and inspiration. At each of these stops, we will uncover a brilliant idea that holds the potential for transforming the places where all of us work. For the most part, they won't be destinations that you might have sought on your own or found in a more traditional book on innovation and business success. Each of these places is intended to stretch your thinking about where great ideas can come from and to give you a powerful sense of what can happen when you commit to walking outside your own world and comfort zone. So if you have an open mind, a spirit of adventure, a burning desire to make a difference, and a pair of comfortable shoes, I sense you'll find a spark of your own genius at each point along the way.

To give you a preview, these 10 journeys will take us:

- Back in time to meet a man with really bad feet and a powerful promise.
- On a walk through a quiet neighborhood with a nine-year-old girl, a special box of cookies, and the magic of a conversation.
- Under a giant tent where the circus and the notion of a performance have been reinvented.
- Into the lobby of a five-star hotel to spend a day in the life of a world-class concierge.
- To one of the world's finest shock trauma centers where life and death decisions are part of a day's work.
- Across the beautiful and harsh terrain of Tanzania to visit the fastest creature on earth.
- To the set of one of the most successful television shows in history, where the nothings in life are cause for celebration.
- Into the unique world of rocket scientists, where their mission demands perfection.
- To the west coast of Sweden and the front-lines of a remarkable effort to make exercise accessible and fun.

And,
- To the comic-book world of one of the most human super-heros to rediscover the amazing power we all possess.

Curious at all? If not, we have a bit more work to do to get you ready.

The notion is quite simple: we are surrounded by brilliant ideas that are there for the taking—with some modification to fit our world and the needs of those we serve. On each trip, we'll visit a compelling concept and wrestle with it as a starting point for thinking in new and powerful ways about your company or organization and its potential. Then you and your colleagues will be challenged to take your own journeys to experience these ideas firsthand, discover what they mean, and figure out how and which ideas to apply to your organization. And you'll have a chance to prove just how curious and smart you really are, and how amazing your company or organization can be.

It is no coincidence that the ideas in this book are drawn from many walks of life. The very nature of innovation and growth suggests that we cast a wide net in searching for clues to success. As a result, they may not be ideas and implications you see instantly, but the process is about opening our minds to possibilities and getting more comfortable with the power of diverse ideas. Of course, not all of these ideas are right for everyone, but most of them should hold powerful seeds for transforming your company or organization.

What drives any successful business or organization is an unwavering commitment to deliver the greatest value to the customers or citizens it serves. In business we get to choose our customers, or at least the ones we would like to be our customers, while in the world of public-sector agencies and nonprofit associations we often have far less say in who will need or demand our services. Whoever our customers turn out to be, our starting point is to understand them and their world more clearly than anyone else. This understanding gives us the context for determining what ideas have the potential to dramatically improve the way we meet their needs.

The challenge is to figure out in our own journeys what is worthy of our curiosity and attention.

This doesn't mean that innovation by creating unique breakthrough ideas is unimportant. In fact, it is essential for economies as a whole and for a small but significant share of companies whose business is focused primarily on cutting-edge technology. These are companies searching for new cures for diseases, newer and better computers, new instruments that can detect threats to our safety, and the list goes on. But even these companies require new approaches and insights to achieve their objectives. In this light, the ten journeys here should serve as equally compelling starting points for their thinking and for the breakthroughs they are trying to achieve.

Curiosity is an innate human gift. We are born with a compelling sense of curiosity that plays itself out until we either touch or taste something we shouldn't or we are told that there are limits to how curious we should be. Now is your chance to shine.

Part Two

Ten Journeys

Dwell in possibility!
—*Emily Dickinson*

Being inexhaustible, life and nature are a
constant stimulus for a creative mind.
—*Hans Hofmann*

Let's set the stage for the journeys that follow by remembering what it was like to take a field trip and how to create the right mindset for unlocking the genius in each of us. To do this, we'll have to go back to our childhoods when field trips were one of the most wonderful parts of going to school. As adults in organizations, we don't take a lot of field trips anymore. In fact, a lot of adults have real difficulty and even anxiety about taking a day off to explore the world around them—unless it means going on a prearranged visit to another company. I am continually surprised by the number of adults on the field trips that we design for companies and organizations who are uncomfortable, at least at the outset, with the experience of going into unfamiliar territory in search of clues and insight. It is not uncommon to have them ask *What is this about?* and *Why in the world are we doing this?* as surrogates for *I can't afford time away from the office* or *This is a weird way to improve our performance,* or *I really don't want to be doing this.* Though by the end of the day, typically they are amazed by the whole experience and their own ability to see and think in new and compelling ways.

But let's get back to our lives as kids for a moment . . .

It's Wednesday at 9:30 AM, and the second graders at Woodlin Elementary School are getting ready for a field trip to the National Building Museum. There they will work with a team of urban planners to design and build a new and better city. It's a big job and a new experience, but it's clear from the energy and enthusiasm in the room that these seven-year-olds are up for the challenge. They've been studying communities for the past month, and now they will have the chance to step out of the classroom and into the real world of learning and creating.

On cue they all get up, tidy their desks, and wait for the commands to grab their coats and lunches, line up, and head to the bus. Without cue, their imaginations take flight. As their teachers and some of their parents guide them down the hall, their heads are filled with a million questions. Will the bus be fancy and play videos? How long will it take to get there? What will happen when we arrive? What will it be like to build a city? How big will our city be? Will we be able to walk around in it? Can we put anything we want in it? Can I live next door to my best friend? Will we be able to bring it back to school? Will we spend the whole day there? Will they give us a snack? Will the snack include soda?

After a thirty-five-minute bus ride, they arrive with eyes wide open as they enter one of the grandest and most remarkable buildings in all of Washington. Once inside they gather around in a circle to meet their teachers for the day and find out how the morning will unfold. They learn how all parts of a city are interrelated and how careful and creative planning can help to build a community that will nurture all of its residents. Then, armed with their assignments, they form small teams to plan and build their part of the city. In a whirlwind of activity, they dive into the cardboard, paint, popsicle sticks, glue, tape, scissors, string, conversations, and other odds and ends that will be the foundation of their creation. City building has begun. In the next hour, magic will unfold in their eyes and in the eyes of all the adults working with them.

If you ask young children what makes a field trip so special, they'll give you some very candid answers:

- "You get to leave school."
- "You don't have to sit at your desk."
- "You get to learn new things in a hands-on way."
- "You think about things differently."
- "You can be as loud as you want."
- "You experience real things instead of things in a book."
- "You get to see and touch things."
- "You get to make new friends."
- "You meet new and different people who are very smart."
- "You use different parts of your brain."
- "You get to get dirty."
- "You get to use your body to learn."
- "You get to see what people are good at."
- "You make something happen."
- "You see your teachers in a different place acting normal."

And it would be hard not to see how each of these special things could benefit adults and the companies and organizations they work in. If you think back on your experiences as a student, it's likely that field trips were an important memory—a wonderful break from sitting at your desk, writing stories, drawing pictures, solving math problems, and the like. They were a chance to learn in the real world with all of its energy and possibilities. They were a chance to make learning come alive, to see the connection between the things you learn in books and the things you learn from experiencing them. Field trips were also a chance to stretch our legs, arms, wings, and imaginations, to see our dreams take flight.

Miss work, walk around, see new things, meet new people, ask a million questions, find new ways of doing things, stretch your thinking, learn, wear yourself out, rediscover the genius in all of us. It is hard to imagine that these basic human abilities are no longer part of our collective comfort zone. Fortunately, we can get them back.

As you read each of the following chapters, I would love for you to think back to your days in school and the magic of field trips. Then I'd love for you to think about what it means to have an open and curious mind. If you can do this, these ten ideas will jump off the page, become much more tangible to you, and even, hopefully, become part of your consciousness about the real keys to customer and business success. Then you and your colleagues can use those open eyes to take your own field trips to really understand each idea and wrestle with how each might apply to you and your organization.

Without shortchanging the discoveries of the world's greatest minds, I'd argue that each of us can be just as brilliant in ways that really matter to the customers we choose to serve. Let's plan to touch base at the end of your travels to see if I'm right.

A Few Important Notes for Your Journeys

The great business philosopher and baseball player Yogi Berra once said, "You can observe a lot simply by watching." However, I would like you and your colleagues to do a bit more. To really understand what is going on in the places you visit, you will have to roll up your sleeves, engage people whenever possible, and ask some good questions. Just what these questions should be will depend on the specific journey, your understanding of what really matters to your customers, your company or organization's compelling focus, and your level of curiosity.

Also, wherever you and your colleagues go, try to understand the ideas that you encounter in their own context. Don't try to instantly translate them to your company or organization. If you do, you'll probably miss much of the magic in them. You'll have plenty of time to sort them out and determine their relevance when you return to the office or wherever you hang out to do your best thinking, share your discoveries, and compare notes. Then you can go through your new collection of possibilities, unlock the best of them, and begin to wrestle with how they might change the equation in your world.

chapter Five

The Power of
a Promise

The Big Idea:
We can succeed in business by guaranteeing satisfaction.

The Journey:
*To an earlier time to visit a man who had a pair of bad feet
and a very different way of looking at customers...*

All great companies and organizations, and some that never
become great, begin with at least one brilliant idea, an idea
that is new, unique, and compelling, and that meets a real need
in a way that no one has before. Typically, the idea is a new
product or service that changes the way we live, work, or play.
But often it is a new way of doing something that changes our
expectations about how things ought to be. In 1912 an entrepreneur and avid sportsman who had a pair of very sensitive feet
would do both. So let's head out to the woods of New England
to meet a remarkable man who had the audacity to believe that
the customer should decide whether he or she was receiving
compelling value from the product that he chose to offer.

1912: Freeport, Maine

His name was Leon Leonwood Bean, and he was—by some accounts—the less-than-enthusiastic manager of a family dry goods business in Freeport, Maine. His clear preference, it seemed, was to go hunting and fishing, a passion that he pursued with great regularity. But keeping his feet dry and comfortable during the wet and snowy months of fall and early winter proved to be a real problem. And try as he might, he could not find a pair of boots that would do the trick.

In the early 1900s, rubber was the only material available that could keep someone or something dry. In fact, the idea of putting rubber soles on footwear had actually been invented by the Mayans sometime in the tenth century. Among the fastest runners of their time, the Mayans actually molded hot liquid rubber around their feet to make a nearly perfect fit. However, rubber boots were not a great option for hiking miles at a time in the back country woods of Maine. So in a moment of inspiration, or possibly desperation, L.L. Bean came up with the idea of stitching a leather top to a rubber shoe bottom, and the Maine Hunting Boot was born. And being enamored with his creation, he soon decided to go into the hunting shoe business.

All great companies and organizations, and some that never become great, begin with at least one brilliant idea.

L.L. Bean launched his new venture the following summer, and the idea seemed to catch on. He quickly sold 100 pairs of the hunting shoes by direct mail to a list of Maine hunting license holders. Not a bad start in a world that at the time was dominated by mail-order giants like Sears, Montgomery Wards, and J.C. Penney. But there was one slight problem. On 90 of these original pairs, the leather tops quickly separated from their rubber bottoms—and the customers quickly asked for a refund. Determined to make the shoes and his fledgling business work, Bean came up with a better design backed by a guarantee "to give satisfaction in every way."

And to affirm his commitment to getting it right every time for every customer, he put the following notice on the wall of his store in Freeport:

NOTICE
I do not consider a sale complete until goods are worn out and customer is still satisfied.

—L.L. Bean, 1916

This combination of an innovative product that met a real customer need and an unconditional guarantee of satisfaction would be the start of a direct-mail empire that is today a household name and one of the most successful and trusted merchants and brands in America. The Maine Hunting Boot can still be found, but with the addition of Gore-Tex®, in the company's famous catalog, on its Web site, and in its retail stores. As for the guarantee, it remains—in even more explicit terms—an essential part of the success of L.L. Bean:

"Our products are guaranteed to give 100% satisfaction in every way. Return anything purchased from us at any time if it proves otherwise. We do not want you to have anything from L.L. Bean that is not completely satisfactory."

Real Guarantees Matter

Doing business as a company, a government agency, or a nonprofit association is really about making a promise to the customers and citizens we choose to serve. It is a promise that we will provide the product, service, solution, or knowledge that really meets their needs. It is also a promise that we will stand behind our offerings with the commitment to make sure they deliver real value—in whatever way we say they will <u>and</u> for as long as a "reasonable" customer might expect them to.

To do this, we must also commit to being very good at what we do. Our ability to design the way our company or organization operates and to put in place the right combination of people, leadership, structure, processes, systems, and values will determine whether our promise amounts to anything. Try to imagine what must go on at L.L. Bean and with its network of suppliers today, as a $2 billion company, in order to back its guarantee. Then try to imagine what you and your organization would have to do to unconditionally guarantee quality, satisfaction, timeliness, responsiveness, competence, reliability, and know-how or whatever else really matters to your customers.

This combination of an innovative product that met a real customer need and an unconditional guarantee of satisfaction would be the start of a direct-mail empire that is today a household name.

We've been talking all along about the importance of being customer-centric, and that's the real power of L.L. Bean's idea. The customer decides whether a pair of hunting boots, a winter coat, or any product Bean offers is worth the price—not at first glance or after a single use, but at any time during the customer's life. No gray area exists. No conditions. No fine print. No time limit. The customer judges the quality and his or her own satisfaction. In L.L. Bean's simple equation, the customer is actually trusted to be an honest partner. Now that's a guarantee. And when you think about the fact that

> **Doing business as a company, a government agency, or a nonprofit association is really about making a promise to the customers and citizens we choose to serve.**

they make stuff that is absolutely going to wear out, their guarantee is even more impressive. So what could be more powerful as the guiding principle of any business or organization than to guarantee what it offers unconditionally and let the customer decide if that equates to what they hoped for? It's hard to imagine something better!

To make this point even clearer, let me give you two more examples of guarantees that exceed customer expectations.

Real Guarantees Change Perceptions

In 1986 Hyundai Motor Company, Korea's largest automaker, entered the U.S. auto market. The company targeted first-time buyers—primarily college students and young families—who needed reliable transportation but did not have a lot of money to spend on a car. Its initial model, the Excel, seemed to fit the bill, setting import car sales records in its first two years. But the Excel wasn't even close to being excellent in terms of quality or design, and it quickly created the perception that Hyundai's cars were cheap and poorly made.

The fact that the cars came from Korea also didn't help matters in the late 1980s. While Japan had earned a reputation for

designing and producing innovative, affordable, and high-quality
products, Korea was still viewed as a second-rate manufacturer.
Failure to overcome these strong perceptions would threaten the
company's ability to survive in America and to expand its product
line over time to larger and more profitable vehicles. Remember
the Yugo? It was Eastern Europe's first foray into the American car
market. This $3,990 vehicle, introduced in 1985, was a PR
marvel and an automotive disaster. Plagued by a host of mechanical problems and poor dealer service, the Yugo quickly found
itself stuck quite literally on the side of the road and relegated to
the scrap heap of U.S. business history.

So imagine the challenge of having to improve the design
and quality of low-cost cars in a market with a growing number
of choices and very little patience for inferior products. Then
imagine the power of a guarantee. In fact, one might argue that
the only way to get potential customers off the dime when they
believe that quality is suspect is to change the equation and guarantee a level of quality that far exceeds their expectations. And
that's just what Hyundai did. It listened carefully to its customers
and critics and committed to improving the way it designed and
built its vehicles. It then committed to back its cars with the
strongest guarantee offered on any car sold in the United
States—10 years or 100,000 miles—more than double the guarantees offered by Toyota, Honda, GM, Ford, Mercedes, BMW,
Lexus, Acura, or any other
premium car maker. It was a
guarantee that would get
attention in the marketplace
and attention on the shop
floor, because making it work would require Hyundai to become
a world-class manufacturer. In 2004 their hard work was reward-
ed when J.D. Power and Associates rated the company's cars

**We must also commit to
being very good at what
we do.**

second to Toyota (and tied with Honda) in initial vehicle quality, higher than every single luxury car brand.

Hyundai's strategy was a stroke of everyday genius. They didn't invent the concept of a guarantee—they just committed to making it better than anyone else in their industry. And they certainly didn't invent the concept of quality—they just committed to raising the bar for low-cost vehicles. When the marketplace doesn't know you, or when it judges your products or services to be inferior, take the risk out of the customer's side of the equation and place it squarely on your own shoulders. At the 2005 Detroit Auto Show, there was great fanfare when Hyundai unveiled its full line of cars and SUVs. It is safe to say that practically everyone who was laughing a few years earlier was now taking notice. Real guarantees can establish credibility and provide a powerful advantage in the most competitive marketplaces. They are a promise to our customers and a challenge to us.

Real Guarantees Change the Game

The power of guarantees doesn't apply only to companies or organizations facing big problems in their markets. It also applies to companies and organizations that are already successful and committed to being the best at what they do. Take the example of Structural Systems, Inc., a regional manufacturer and distributor of structural components that are used to build houses. Founded in 1968, Structural Systems produces roof trusses and floor and wall systems for some of America's leading home builders. They also sell engineered wood products such as floor joists, windows, and doors. They've established a great reputation for designing and building these components to the exact specifications of their customers. But they're also in a very competitive industry in which price, quality, reliability, and timing are the biggest parts of the buying equation. So where does a powerful guarantee fit in?

For builders, time is money. Development projects and individual houses are built on a carefully orchestrated schedule. When the schedule slips, problems arise, and extra costs are incurred. Components need to arrive at just the right time to ensure that houses go up and are ready when they are promised to buyers. In a booming market, however, builders are often forced to base their schedule on the production capability of their partners, a capability that often means an eight-week or longer lead time from when an order is placed

Try to imagine what you and your organization would have to do to unconditionally guarantee quality, satisfaction, timeliness, responsiveness, competence, reliability, and know-how.

to when the components arrive at the job site—without any guarantee of the actual delivery date. But what if a company could reduce lead time *and* guarantee a delivery date that matched the builder's schedule perfectly? That would be hard to beat. And that's exactly what Structural Systems decided to do. In fact, they committed to stand their industry on its head by cutting production time in half and guaranteeing delivery within four weeks. To accomplish this, they assembled a team of everyday geniuses representing each of the key functions in the production and delivery process. Although none of them bore much of a resemblance to Einstein, each was an expert on his or her part of the company's operations, and each was passionate about the potential for the business to be brilliant.

The team was given sixty days to reinvent the way they did business by redesigning their internal processes and systems and by rethinking the way they collaborated with each other and with their customers. Central to their new approach was a real partnership with each customer. If the customer could commit to providing complete and accurate information within five days of placing any order, Structural Systems could commit to designing, building, and delivering it to the highest standards within the remaining 15 days—and providing an unconditional guarantee. The team met their deadline, tested the new processes with key customers, worked out the glitches, and began offering their guarantee—and immediately saw the benefits. In the first twelve months, the company met its four-week promise over 99 percent of the time. It is probably no coincidence that their sales increased by more than 50 percent in that same time period. Real guarantees change expectations and shake up old notions and entire industries. They help to set apart companies or organizations and fuel their growth. The challenge for Structural Systems is to build even greater value tied to its guarantee to maintain success in a tighter market.

> **When the marketplace doesn't know you, or when it judges your products or services to be inferior, take the risk out of the customer's side of the equation and place it squarely on your own shoulders.**

Guarantees Challenge Us to Get It Right

But isn't it easy to guarantee manufactured products? After all, Coleman offers a 100-year warranty on its top-of-the-line stainless steel coolers, and Le Creuset, the renowned French cookware manufacturer, offers a lifetime guarantee on its nonstick pots and pans. And a host of other well-known and less-known companies offer a wide range of unconditional product guarantees that last for some incredible period of time, or guarantees

that offer their customers a full refund if they are not completely satisfied. But no one buys a product hoping for a full refund.
What we want are products that actually work. Real guarantees
are about the underlying quality and value that goes into what a
company or organization offers, not the customer's recourse if
that quality and value are lacking.

Given this, real guarantees are the exception rather than the
rule. If you have a problem with most products before they have
provided reasonable value, feel free to talk with a manager dis-
creetly, and he or she might be willing to make an accommoda-
tion. That's a promise they
can stand behind as long as
they aren't forced to put it in
writing, or as long as it is
backed by the necessary fine
print, drafted by the best
lawyers that money can buy, explaining the conditions of their
unconditional guarantee. Looking for something that won't last
very long? Try buying a product without a guarantee or one with
a guarantee worthy of laughter. I'd be sure to use it quickly if I
were you . . . they probably know something about the quality
and value that went into it.

**Real guarantees change
expectations and shake up
old notions and entire
industries.**

Take a look at the latest in computers and consumer electronics. These products are high on technology, but low on the
commitment of their makers to ensure reliability. In fact, the
recent trend is moving toward 30-day guarantees. After that you
can pay extra for extended coverage based on your estimation of
when the product will fall apart and the manufacturer's estimation of how many will fall apart and what it will cost to fix them.
That is pretty darned impressive. Why not build products better
and back them longer? Remember when household appliances
were designed to last almost forever? You might still have an old

refrigerator in the basement that's chugging along after 25 years. But today, the second word out of a typical salesperson's mouth is: "Would you like to protect your investment with our fabulous extended-warranty plan?" No. I'd like to buy a product that is actually worth my investment! I'd like someone to really stand behind their products with a guarantee that means something.

More and more service organizations are seeing the power of unconditional guarantees as the best way to ensure value and differentiate their offerings in ways that matter most to customers. Some training companies offer customers their money back if they aren't completely satisfied with the educational experience. In the process, they are actually challenging themselves to create offerings that are worth something. Some Web design firms promise that you won't have to pay unless you are 100 percent satisfied. Could it be that they have done their homework and have the right skills, experience, and process to meet most customer expectations? Hotels guarantee to provide a clean room or you don't have to pay. Retail stores offer a lowest price guarantee to attract customers. Restaurants offer free lunch if your food isn't delivered in five minutes. (If they would only combine that with the promise of a delicious and healthy meal.) Dry cleaners offer to clean your garment again until they get the spot out (or possibly destroy your favorite pants?). Repair companies guarantee when their technicians will arrive and how long it will take to fix the problem. Local governments offer to respond to citizens' inquiries within 24 hours. Somewhere in all of these promises is a chance to deliver greater value to their customers. It is a chance to

They are actually challenging themselves to create offerings that are worth something.

guarantee the aspect of what they offer that matters most and, in the process, dramatically improve the way they do business.

Like their counterparts in product companies, the best service organizations must also understand the world of their customers and their own business better than anyone else. Based on this knowledge, they too design the way they operate to assure real value by putting in place the best possible combination of people, leadership, structure, processes, systems, and core values. They know that no guarantee can cover a promise unfulfilled. They also know that a guarantee backed by real results is their not-so-secret weapon in the battle to compete *and* that meaningful guarantees can be structured to address practically anything that really matters to customers. Beyond service quality, guarantees can make a compelling difference in promising a level of performance, reliability, cost, cost of use, response time, speed of delivery, knowledge to support the use of a service, and a host of other things yet to be determined by your imagination, skill, and the needs of your customers. The upside is huge. But a promise is also a chance to screw up big time. Just take a look at your own industry.

What Is Your Promise?

Let's turn our attention to your company or organization and the promise it makes to its customers. To do this, we have to ask a few essential questions. First, what's your compelling value proposition? Second, does your value proposition really matter to customers? Third, does your value proposition give you a real and sustainable edge in the marketplace? Fourth, how do you back up your promise? Next, take a minute to write down your guarantee as clearly as possible—whether it is explicit, implicit, or a fall-back position when things don't turn out as planned.

Before you get comfortable (or uncomfortable) with your guarantee, I'd like to push your thinking a bit. We started this chapter by visiting with an everyday genius with bad feet. Bean turned out to be brilliant, and I believe that you and your colleagues can be too. His greatest contribution to business and organizations was, as we've discussed, the notion of unconditional customer satisfaction, and I'd like you to see how your company or organization stacks up against the promise he made to his customers. So look at what you've

We have found that one of the best ways to figure how to be great at something is to begin by figuring out how to be awful at it.

written down and think about whether our new friend L.L. Bean would be impressed. If you answered *yes,* you're halfway home. The field trip you are about to take will help to strengthen your already strong position in the market. If you answered *no,* the initial field trip will present a very important challenge.

In helping our customers to differentiate themselves in ways that make a powerful and lasting difference in their markets, we often take the time to have fun with concepts like an unconditional guarantee of satisfaction. We have found that one of the best ways to figure how to be great at something is to begin by figuring out how to be awful at it. To do this, we wander around looking for impossible claims and "worst" practices that can be put together in ways that would strike fear in the hearts and minds of customers. So before I send you on your initial field trip to explore the promise and potential of offering a guarantee that means something, let me share a few *not-so-great ones* developed just for fun on field trips with a few of our customers.

A manufacturing firm developed this amazing promise as a starting point for challenging their thinking about the right guarantee:

"It's the Amazing Intergalactic Coffee Wizard—a true marvel of European design, space age technology, and turbocharged caffeine enjoyment. Just plug it into your desktop or laptop computer, follow a few simple software commands, and you'll be brewing perfect coffee instantly. No need to add anything. The Wizard comes with its own lifetime supply of fresh spring water. And if you're one of the lucky ones, the Coffee Wizard could give months or possibly a year of trouble-free service. In fact, we're so confident of its durability and value that we back it unconditionally for a full 30 days—with only a few

> **When we stand behind what we offer with our full commitment, we are able to bring to bear so much skill, purpose, and passion that no one can beat us.**

very minor exceptions (that are described in detail in the attached waiver of liability). But don't worry. If you want to make sure it keeps brewing without skipping a beat, you can buy one of our stupendous extended service plans. For only $139 we'll protect your purchase for an entire year. Please specify if you have a PC or a Mac when ordering."

An industrial service provider came up with the following service offer:

"At Perfect Heating and Cooling, we strive to get the job done right the first time. Our self-trained technicians, antiquated diagnostic equipment, and wavering commitment to excellence will have you warm or cold in no time. And if this wasn't enough, we back it up with our exclusive one-hour written guarantee. If your system fails to operate after we try to fix it or if it cuts off again before our technician can get away from your premises, we'll stay and try again. And we'll keep on trying until we get it fixed, break your furnace in a million pieces, or aggravate you so much that you decide to call the police. We also offer our patent pending 'Gold Key' annual service agreement—the ultimate in homeowner protection. For a single fixed fee of $2,800, we'll send everyone in our company to your home every week for an entire year. We'll even clean up the mess we make unless we're in a hurry. And if you're one of the first ten callers, you'll receive a year of fake fireplace logs. So call now—operators are standing by."

Who said coming up with brilliant (or brilliantly bad ideas) had to be difficult? Armed with these pathetic offerings, each of these organizations went into the world around them to uncover clues for creating unique and powerful guarantees. You and your team can do the same thing. In fact, you might want to get your colleagues together and come up with your own worst-case guarantee as a fun way to prepare for your time in the field. Then meet me at the front of the building because it's time to get out and discover a world of great ideas, insights, and possibilities.

Take Your Own Journey

Your assignment on this initial field trip is pretty straightforward, and it should be a lot of fun. Ideas about how to guarantee satisfaction abound. All you'll need to find them is an open mind, a sense of curiosity, a keen desire to take your organization to new heights, a good map and a pair of very comfortable shoes. Your objective is to find as many great examples of powerful guarantees as you can in a single work day. To do this, you and your colleagues will have to search high and low across your community to uncover companies and organizations that make and keep amazing promises to their customers. You'll probably have to split up into smaller working groups so you can cast a wider net over a sea of possibilities. You might already have some ideas about how to get started and where to look first. After all, you're probably familiar with a number of world-class companies that stand behind their offerings. However, I realize this is the first field trip I'm sending you on, so in case you're stuck, here are three great places to get started . . .

The World's Most Admired Companies.

Grab the latest *Fortune* magazine list of the world's most admired companies and pick four or five with offices or locations in your community. Or, quickly put together your own list of the most admired companies operating in your area, based on the knowledge and experiences of members of your team. Then head out to learn about them firsthand. If possible, try to talk with some of their employees and customers so you can understand what makes these businesses so special. Then try to put yourself in their customers' shoes. It is a safe bet that most of these companies prosper by making a compelling promise to their customers. If they aren't one of your competitors, they should be delighted to talk with you.

The World of Nonprofit and Public Sector Organizations.

Think about all of the nonprofit and governmental organizations that are pillars in your community. These could be philanthropic organizations, leading museums, theaters, the orchestra, the ballet, a local sports team, the library, a university, or a leading hospital. Each of these organizations, in its own way, makes a powerful promise to those they serve. Their promises could provide a different and important way of looking at value and the power of guarantees. Again, pick four of five of these organizations to visit and learn about. Then try to figure out their unique role in the community and their guarantee.

Get Lost on Purpose.

There is a lot to be said for random acts of insight and going almost anywhere with your eyes wide open. Pick another part or aspect of town that is filled with energy and activity and walk up and down its streets looking for brilliant ideas and powerful guarantees. Look on signs and billboards or the pages of the local newspaper for clues of companies and organizations that are making bold promises. Then track them down and try to find out as much as you can about them. Who knows what you will stumble onto?

Real guarantees challenge us to be better in ways that transform our own businesses and relationships with customers. They also challenge us to bring out the genius in all of our people. When we stand behind what we offer with our full commitment, we are able to bring to bear so much skill, purpose, and passion that no one can beat us. Keeping meaningful promises is the foundation of a long and prosperous venture.

In case you haven't guessed already, I stand in awe of that guy who many years ago used a pair of sensitive feet, a set of great values, and a bit of genius to spark this quiet revolution.

chapter Six

The Magic of a Conversation

The Big Idea:
*We can succeed in business by having conversations
that really matter.*

The Journey:
*A walk through the neighborhood with a nine-year-old girl
and a remarkable box of cookies . . .*

"Talk is cheap." "Actions speak louder than words." "Just do
it!" "Go ahead, make my day!"

We live in a world of action whether it is the right action or
not. That's not necessarily a bad thing. If we want to compete
and win in business today, we have to be capable of figuring out
the right things to do and do them faster and better than anyone else. We also have to begin and continue the process by having the right conversations with those we choose to serve. Yet it
seems as though we've lost a sense of the necessity and potential
of conversations that matter—conversations that create a compelling connection, build a stronger relationship, and enable us
to deliver real value.

If we are salespeople, the challenge is even greater. So imagine what we could learn from people who bring a conversation that almost everyone longs for. It's one that comes with very few strings attached and a fair share of calories—though they rarely produce guilt. So let's visit a few neighbors, swing by a few offices, or set up a booth outside the local supermarket to discover what's really inside a three-dollar-and-fifty-cent box of Girl Scout cookies and the simple magic of the conversation that comes with them.

Silver Spring, Maryland

It will probably not come as any great surprise to you that most customers and potential customers do not eagerly await the arrival of salespeople unless they have an urgent need for a product, service, or solution. Or unless those salespeople are Girl Scouts! Beyond the obvious, why do highly trained professionals selling the latest and greatest stuff strike fear in the hearts of most buyers while untrained kids selling a 75-year-old tradition are welcomed with open arms?

The best way to answer this question is to actually spend a January evening following a Girl Scout around the neighborhood, something my wife and I have had the pleasure of doing with our daughters for the past eight years.

Somewhere around the three-hundredth box, and the fifth evening of hitting the pavement, I realized something magic was happening. Carly, an extremely outgoing and downright amusing nine-year-old, would knock on doors and receive the type of welcome that salespeople, political candidates, and people on a religious mission could only dream of. At each

I seems as though we've lost a sense of the necessity and potential of conversations that matter.

door it seemed, the residents would see her enthusiastic grin and break into their biggest smiles, saying, "Carly, I was hoping you'd be back!" or "Carly, I thought it was getting to be cookie time again," or "Hi, I'm so glad you're here. I was afraid I'd missed Girl Scout cookie season." "Don't worry," Carly would reply, "I'd never forget you guys." Then followed a quick round of catching up:

"Please come in."
"Do you have a few minutes?"
"You're getting so big!"
"How's school?"
"How are your mom and dad?"
"How are your sister and brother?"
"How is your dog? Is she still a puppy?"

To which Carly would quickly answer, "She's not really a puppy anymore, but she thinks she is. And she weighs 92 pounds now, which is awfully big for a puppy!"

"I remember the first time I bought cookies from your sister Sara," the neighbor would continue. "I can't believe she's at Blair (High School) now."

"And she's even in the marching band," Carly would respond.

"What instrument does she play?"

"Clarinet, but she wants to play the drums. She's very good at music, but she's having a bit of trouble with the marching part."

"Was that your brother I saw racing down the street on a skateboard the other day?" they would continue.

"You mean the crazy kid who is trying to break every bone in his body? Yup, that's Noah!"

"Well, come in and make yourself comfortable. Would you like a cup of hot chocolate or a glass of milk?"

"Sure. Hot chocolate is my favorite! (pause) With marshmallows?"

"Okay. Now, show me what you have this year. Anything new that I should know about?"

Carly, being the skilled salesperson she is, would then begin the formal "selling" part of the conversation by recalling what each neighbor (a.k.a. customer) had purchased last year.

"Of course, we have thin mints," might be the starting point. "And I know you like them a lot. And we have a new flavor this year called 'Café Cookies' that are pretty good for grown-ups. You can dip them in coffee or tea or hot chocolate. They're not so sweet, and they don't have too many calories."

"I'll have my usual five boxes of Thin Mints, and I'll also try a box of the Café Cookies." "Great," replies Carly, jotting down the order. "And the All Abouts are good too if you like chocolate. They even have information about the Girl Scouts written right on the cookie."

"Okay, I'll take a box of those as well. And what about the Lemon Coolers?"

"Kind of boring if you ask me," Carly would respond, "other than the powdered sugar on the outside."

"You're probably right. We'll stick with what we've got."

"Sounds good to me," Carly would conclude as she finished her order-taking notations on the full-color order forms adorned with scrumptious pictures of the products. Then she would tidy up her mess, thank her hosts for their order and their kindness, and begin to make her way to the door. While Carly always enjoyed the time spent with each of her adoring fans, she knew that her sales commissions were dependent on working her way through the neighborhood. The trick was to balance a desire to reconnect with her customers with the need for speed. Then armed with her amazing smile, uncanny product knowledge, uncontrollable honesty, and the promise of cookies to be delivered in a couple of weeks, Carly would say good night and head up the street, bringing joy and racking up sales.

If we want to compete and win in business today, we have to be capable of figuring out the right things to do and do them faster and better than anyone else.

The scene at the first house would be repeated at the second, third, fourth, and so on until Carly had either run out of steam or passed her 8:00 PM cookie-selling curfew.

It is safe to say that the experience at almost every house struck a powerful cord with neighbors. For some it was probably a connection with their own childhood. The Girl Scouts estimate that more than 50 million girls have been scouts since the founding of the organization in 1912, so there is a reasonable chance that the person opening the door was either a Girl Scout or the sibling or parent of one. For others, it was probably a connection to a simple and more hopeful time when neighborhood and community were at the center of our lives and the world was a lot slower and less complicated. For others, it was probably a refreshing pause to acknowledge the kindness and magic of childhood, something that most adults too often lose touch with. For still others, it was probably the belief that the money was going to a good cause and a willingness to support the Girl Scouts, an organization with strong and compelling values and a commitment to the positive development of girls. And for a few, it might simply be the cookies.

In case you haven't purchased Girl Scout Cookies recently, let me catch you up on a few of the basics. First, there are currently eight delicious flavors:

Current Types of Girl Scout Cookies	
Cookie	**Key Ingredient(s)**
All Abouts	Fudge bottom, Information about scouting
Café Cookies	Cinnamon spice
Do-si-dos	Oatmeal, peanut butter crème
Lemon Coolers	Lemon, powdered sugar
Samoas	Toasted coconut, chocolate, chewy stuff
Tagalongs	Peanut butter, chocolate
Thin Mints	Peppermint, chocolate
Trefoils	Shortbread

*Source: Girl Scout Cookie® boxes and promotional materials

Each flavor comes in a fun and up-to-date package that shows Girl Scouts in action with a focus on the healthy lifestyle of being a scout—having fun; helping others; building strong minds, bodies, and character; building strong friendships, leadership skills, and community; and living, it would seem, in a world that is at odds with so much of today's reality and yet encompasses many of our hopes for the future.

In purely economic terms, each box of Girl Scout Cookies costs $3.50, a percentage of which goes to the troop selling them to be used to support programs and activities. While it is difficult to get an exact sales figure, one recent estimate put gross cookie revenue for 2006 at well over a half billion dollars. While each of the eight cookies seems to sell reasonably well, Thin Mints are the most popular type, accounting for up to 50 percent of sales in some areas. Their fans enjoy them at room temperature or frozen.

It will probably not come as any great surprise to you that most customers and potential customers do not eagerly await the arrival of salespeople.

At the risk of heresy, I must admit that Girl Scout Cookies are not the most delicious cookies in the world. Homemade cookies made from scratch have got them beat. So do cookies from a great bakery. Even some prepackaged cookies of more sophisticated pedigrees can be quite a bit more delicious. But what makes the purchase of Girl Scout Cookies most significant for those of us who run a business, or any organization that requires us to make a sale, is the nature of the conversation that this product and its undersized sales force invite.

So somewhere between the Dirdas', the Maklans', the Ackermans', and the Winarskys' house, it dawned on me: the cookies mattered but not nearly as much as the nature and content of the conversations they inspired. Were most of us having the wrong conversations with our customers all along? If so, should we turn to the Girl Scouts instead of another training program on "spin selling," or "consultative selling," or the "sales secrets of the masters," or "key account selling," or any one of a thousand courses on the keys to sales and business success?

It is worth noting that most, if not all, of the people (i.e., girls) selling Girl Scout Cookies have little or no formal sales training, and that is probably part of their charm. They also receive very modest compensation, which is entirely commission based. Each year a set of prizes or rewards is available depending on the level of sales generated by each salesperson. These rewards are relatively modest given the effort involved. For example, selling 250 boxes of cookies might be enough to earn a large stuffed animal toy or a beanbag chair. The big reward comes to the troop. However, most of the girls, especially the younger ones, are excited about these prizes.

I should also point out that in addition to neighborhood sales, Girl Scout troops make arrangements to sell cookies outside local supermarkets, office supply stores, and other high-traffic locations. In these places, they typically set up a modest booth (i.e., a card table with a homemade sign) and then engage passersby with their compelling appeal. As with door-to-door sales, there is a clear focus on neighborliness. These are girls from the local community who represent an institution that strikes a cord in the minds and hearts of neighbors.

Conversations Matter

Conversations matter in a way that we must all understand if we want to remain relevant to the customers we choose to serve. And conversations that matter enable us to connect with our customers and potential customers in a compelling way. They allow us to get beyond the surface, to know our customers better, and to have them know us better as individuals and organizations. Conversations that matter enable us to find out what is going on in our customer's world, what concerns them, what excites them, how their needs are evolving and what they believe is possible. This allows us to figure out the best way to meet their needs by delivering value that matters.

Part of what makes a Girl Scout's conversation so compelling is the fact that it happens on a regular basis—in their case, once a year. It returns just like the seasons. It is a ritual that, while it lasts for only a few moments, merits engagement and celebration. A ritual that suggests we care, that we have not forgotten those we choose to serve. Once a year is probably not often enough for most of our relationships, but the regular

The trick was to balance a desire to reconnect with her customers with the need for speed.

and ritual aspects are vital to making and maintaining conversations that matter.

Remember the classic United Airlines commercial from several years ago that targeted anyone who depends on building lasting customer relationships? In it, a company's boss calls his troops together in a glass conference room to make a solemn confession. One of their oldest customers has decided to change vendors after 20 years of doing business because he no longer feels a sense of connection.

"We used to do business with a handshake," the boss laments. "Face to face. Now it's a phone call and a fax. Get back to you later with another fax probably. Well, folks, something's got to change. That's why we're going to set out for a little face-to-face chat with every customer we have."

When a team member reminds him that this will mean going to more than 200 cities, the boss quickly says that he doesn't care, as he begins handing out plane tickets. The last one will be his own ticket to visit the old customer.

Obviously, having meaningful conversations was (and still is) good business for airlines like United. But the commercial and its message are compelling.

My premise here, as it is in every journey in this book, is that customers long for greater value and more meaning from the relationships they have with those who choose to serve them. If we aren't providing that meaning and value, they have no great need to interact with us or continue to do business with us, and they certainly have no great need to waste time with our salespeople. They can decide to walk with a phone call, a fax, an e-mail, or no word at all.

The trend in companies and organizations today, however, is toward fewer and fewer real conversations. We are either too busy, don't believe it is that important, or have lost the interest and ability to speak to the folks who matter most. We send e-mail and text messages, made even more cryptic by the requirements of our BlackBerry and Treo devices, as though they were a real substitute for conversation. We are short and to the point. No real warmth or curiosity. Just the facts. We seem to have forgotten how to write or interact with any real passion, even though that is what life is all about.

Conversations that matter enable us to find out what is going on in our customer's world, what concerns them, what excites them, how their needs are evolving and what they believe is possible.

When we do speak, it is often to exchange voicemail as though our messages and perpetual phone tag constitute a dialogue of substance. We even turn to teleconferences with growing popularity because it is quicker and cheaper than getting together, although it is not nearly as productive or meaningful. But the cost of our travel time and the cost of travel itself provide more than ample justification. In many cases, that makes sense, but not when it comes to building and maintaining real customer relationships.

So we simply get together less! Imagine how this new phenomenon has even crept into our busy social lives. People now shop online, make arrangements and reservations online, attend seminars and other events online, and even date by computer without ever getting together face to face. One can only imagine that soon prayer and lifecycle events such as baptisms, bar and bat mitzvahs, confirmations, weddings, and even funerals will be available by podcast.

Customers long for greater value and more meaning from the relationships they have with those who choose to serve them.

So against this depersonalized backdrop, the Girl Scouts ask us to slow down and chat face to face, to notice the small and big changes that occurred during the year, to take stock of the past 12 months as though they matter, to be open, honest, and caring—as conversations of and with children invariably are—to notice what is different and what is the same, and to imagine what is possible over a box of cookies.

Conversations that matter require people to be engaged, to honestly care about each other more than about any financial return, to commit to knowing and understanding better, and to sharing information, insights, and questions of value. And to be capable of meaningful conversations with those we serve, we need to be capable of having them with each other in our own companies and organizations. We need to think of our organizations as places built on the value of conversation.

It probably will not surprise you to realize that some companies and organizations are all about having or facilitating conversations that matter. It is an essential part of their formula for success. While the folks at Starbucks sell coffee plus other beverages and food to go with it, they are really the most recent embodiment of a centuries-old tradition of coffeehouses that probably began in the Middle East, in cities like Baghdad and Tehran. These coffeehouses not only offer refreshment but also serve as hangouts for conversation, reading, writing, playing games, and now Web-surfing. So while their business focuses on refreshment, the environment they have created and reproduced in thousands of locations around the globe was until recently really all about creating a comfortable place for conversation—in essence, for maintaining a tradition as old as time.

Many of us joke that there is now a Starbucks on every corner, and walking through the streets of many cities it certainly seems that way. And that may end up being their undoing. But that is not much different than life and business was in an earlier point in time. In the first half of the 1700s, there were more than 500 coffeehouses in the city of London alone. There were also more than 60,000 pubs in England which

We seem to have forgotten how to write or interact with any real passion, even though that is what life is all about.

traced their history back more than 2,000 years as places where neighbors and villagers also gathered to talk, conduct business, possibly trade cows for magic beans, play games, and on occasion get drunk. They were places where you belonged as part of the community and where no one was ever considered a stranger.

But the folks at Starbucks and their competitors, such as Caribou and Tully's, are not the only companies that recognize the power of the Girl Scouts' formula. Think about State Farm, one of the largest property and automobile insurance companies in North America. They must be doing something right to hold their market position for such a long time. Supporting their success is the simple notion that is embodied in their motto: "Like a good neighbor, State Farm is there." Their roots and headquarters in the neighborly Midwestern city of Bloomington, Illinois, seem to bear this out.

Is State Farm Insurance more neighborly than its competitors when it comes to delivering value? It is hard to be certain. There are

We need to think of our organizations as places built on the value of conversation.

many insurance companies that receive high marks for responding to the needs of their customers. But State Farm's history is one built on compelling examples of employees who were committed to having conversations that matter with neighbors who happened to be customers. Those conversations were about understanding needs, demonstrating caring, and bringing something of value, and often that value meant going above and beyond the expected call of duty.

Today, as more people become more mobile, the challenge of being a good neighbor gets harder. But even if we can't be an actual neighbor who is just around the corner, we can bring to bear the special feeling of neighborliness for the customers we choose to serve. You may have a particular Starbucks where you hang out in your hometown. So when you're on the road or when you move, you will probably seek out a Starbucks to replicate the sense of neighborhood and community that comes with their daily fix of caffeine. If you move to a new community, you can presume that the new State Farm agent is committed to being a good neighbor. And, when the doorbell rings and a new girl scout appears, you will probably decide that she—like her "sister" in your hometown—warrants your kindness and interest. She is the keeper of the flame that we so desperately want or need to continue.

Do Your Conversations Matter?

So what is the conversation you have with your customers and prospects? Does it create a sense of a simpler, more honest, and meaningful relationship that you commit to bring to each and every one of them? Is it something that matters, filled with expectation and the promise of value? Or is it simply the minimum daily requirement for hopefully keeping your relationship alive?

What if your customers and prospects couldn't wait to see you again? What if they longed to catch up over a cup of hot chocolate, to see how you've been doing, to admire how you've grown, and to find out what new things you had to offer? "What did I buy last year? I'll have the same and more." What if the conversation brought out the best in both of you?

As you take this journey, think about the power of a conversation. Then think about whether or not it matters in your world and the lessons you and your colleagues could learn from taking a walk around the neighborhood with a nine-year-old girl and a box of cookies. What are the possibilities of a conversation? Like the challenge presented in the last chapter, you might also want to think about how to create the worst possible conversations as a way to quickly get back on track.

Take Your Own Journey

Now take your own journey. Conversations that matter can be found in all aspects of our lives, and so can conversations that don't matter. Your objective here is to find as many great examples of conversations that matter as you can in a single work day. To do this, you and your colleagues will have to search high and low across your community to uncover companies and organizations that strike a real chord in the hearts and minds of those they serve. Some will be businesses, but many more will come from other walks of life, such as schools and educational institutions, nonprofit and volunteer organizations that are eager to enlist people's support to make a difference in the community, houses of worship, and so on. You'll probably have to split up into smaller working groups so you can cast a wider net over a sea of possibilities. In fact, you might already have some ideas about how to get started and where to look first.

I'm not going to give you too many more specifics in this chapter because I want you to start stretching your own thinking.

Real conversations challenge us to be better in ways that transform our own businesses and our relationships

Even if we can't be an actual neighbor who is just around the corner, we can bring to bear the special feeling of neighborliness for the customers we choose to serve.

with customers. They also challenge us to bring out the genius in all of our people. When we commit to communicating with customers and each other, we are able to bring to bear so much skill, purpose, and passion that no one can beat us. Conversations that matter are an essential part of the foundation for long and prosperous relationships.

In case you haven't guessed already, I am an easy target for Girl Scouts selling cookies. There is something about the magic, simple honesty, and everyday genius of the conversation they bring, combined with my love of sugar, that makes an unbeatable combination.

chapter seven

The Wonder of a Performance

The Big Idea:
We can win in business by creating a compelling performance.

The Journey:
Under the big top to a performance of Cirque du Soleil . . .

Whether we realize it or not, our organizations spend each and every day performing, and the quality of our performance determines our success. Most of us rarely think of our work as a show, our strategy and tactics as the script, our colleagues as performers, or our facilities and physical assets as the stage and props. And we rarely think of the customers as the audience or even some of the participants. However, our ability to create a performance that delivers compelling value by inspiring the customer could be the key to our ongoing success. Imagine what we could learn by spending time with the people who literally reinvented one of the most renowned ideas in the history of performance. Imagine spending an evening with the people who have reinvented the circus and in the process created one of the most successful entertainment companies in the world.

2002: Sydney, Australia

The lights go down, the crowd settles in, and a man of somewhat unusual appearance enters the arena. His name is
Monsieur Fleur, a somewhat short and oddly shaped fellow
dressed in black pants, red velvet jacket, oversized bowtie, and
simple hat. He is carrying a large staff befitting a fool who
believes he is a king. Monsieur Fleur will be our guide through
this performance. "Alegria!" he shouts, announcing that the
show and the world of the next ninety minutes is about to
begin. Then, as the music builds, he makes his way into the
audience, creating an initial source of amusement and questions
for the people he passes. He picks out a member of the audience, a tall slender man wearing a business suit, and grasps his

arm gently, lifting him out of his seat to be taken backstage. Everyone, including his wife, is left to wonder how and when the man will return.

Then Monsieur Fleur sits down in the man's chair for a moment before heading onstage. In this brief encounter, he has engaged the audience in the show. Although they will still be observers of the performance, the wall that separates them from the performers has been broken. They have been taken in. Now on to the show . . .

This is the circus reinvented. Cirque du Soleil—or Circus of the Sun—is an amazing fusion of the circus's varied forms, centuries of street performance, and a host of other types of performances from around the world. It features amazing acrobatics, incredible aerial exhibitions, feats of daring involving fire, unbelievable tumbling and gymnastics, and tests of unimaginable balance, flexibility, and remarkable strength, as well as clowns, mimes, and illusion. It offers unforgettable characters wearing dazzling costumes, striking sets and set changes that seem to appear out of thin air, bold and dramatic music and lighting, and special effects that challenge the senses. It wraps around a story that is likely to address

Our ability to create a performance that delivers compelling value by inspiring the customer could be the key to our ongoing success.

one or more of the basic themes of human existence in a world filled with issues and challenges—themes of struggle, change, the coming of age, finding our place in a new order of things, hope amid fear, and love and longing in an unforgiving world.

The real purpose of the story is to provide the glue or context for the remarkable parts of the performance that flow in rapid succession. In Cirque du Soleil's "Alegria," these elements are the:

- Synchronized Trapeze—two aerialist performers twist, turn, and fly in unison, appearing to defy the laws of gravity and sanity.
- Fast Track—an awesome trampoline emerges from under the stage, and The Bronx, a gang that represents the next generation, demonstrates great strength and grace.
- Fire-Knife Dance—to the pounding rhythm of Congo drums, a strong and daring tribal performer weaves one and then two flaming knives around his body with increasing speed, complexity, and danger.
- Hoops—a graceful young woman performs a seemingly impossible display of rhythmic gymnastics, contortion, and balance assisted by a set of silver hoops.
- Strong Man—a big hulking man with an attention-grabbing growl demonstrates acts of superhuman strength.
- Flying Man—a lone artist seems to defy gravity by flying around the stage holding onto a single rope as he performs unbelievable aerial feats.
- Russian Bars—acrobats are flung into the air from a set of narrow bars resting on the shoulders of catchers. In the air they do an incredible set of twists, flips, and synchronized somersaults.
- Contortion—a birdlike woman/child demonstrates amazing feats of balance and flexibility as she moves effortlessly between poses.
- Aerial High Bar—a group of daring acrobats flies high above the stage, seemingly defying death as they swing and catch each other before finally plunging onto a net below.

Interspersed among these acts or elements are other fascinating characters. A group of remarkable clowns, including one with only a tuft of blond hair on his head, offers a real juxtaposition to the other almost unbelievable performers. In their brief moments in the spotlight, they convey the most basic of human emotions—humor and joy, fear and sadness. One moment a clown is mimicking the fire-knife dance with a single candle to show us a somewhat extreme fear of fire, and the next moment he mimics the flying man by showing his discomfort with leaving earth's firm footing. At

What makes a performance compelling is its ability to transport the audience to another place filled with wonder and possibilities.

another time he is trapped in a dangerous storm whipped up in dramatic fashion almost instantly onstage. The clowns provide the underlying feelings that all of us share and often avoid confronting.

Along with Monsieur Fleur, there are two other guides of sorts called the Singer in White and the Singer in Black. Throughout the show, we hear their beautiful and haunting singing in a unique language that sounds like a fusion of French, Italian, English, and perhaps other tongues. They add to the experience without our knowing exactly what they are saying. Maybe it is so we can be free to let them say whatever the performance moves us to hear.

There are other characters, such as the nostalgic Old Birds who look more like chickens after an uncontrolled scientific experiment. They waddle around the stage observing, with some concern and confusion, a world that is tilting quickly toward the young. The Angels represent the youth of the future, and Tamir and Little Tamir, who are Asian-looking clowns, seem to embody kindness. The latter are keen observers and helpers who are constantly curious and smiling.

At the end of all the acts/performance elements, the grand finale brings all the characters to form one unified team—no one more remarkable than the rest except in the eyes of the beholder.

This point is reinforced when those who have been wearing masks remove them to reveal the faces of real people just like us. In fact, this theme of everyone's role having value and importance is carried throughout the entire show. Even when the main performers are engaging the audience, the other characters seem equally engaged and worthy of at least some of our attention. Even if they are simply sitting in the corner of the stage smiling at the wonders of their colleagues.

To make these performances go off without a hitch requires the right planning, the right people, and the right practice.

Cirque du Soleil is an international phenomenon, a wildly successful and creative fusion of a world of performance that is itself a new form of art. Its performances have captivated audiences around the globe, engaging the senses, and challenging people to think about what is possible. The origins of Cirque du Soleil and its remarkable creativity and business success have been recounted in many articles, but that is not really our purpose here. Instead it is the notion of creating a compelling performance that is the heart of this journey. As you can tell from the description, Cirque du Soleil is all about superlatives.

Rethinking a History of Performance

To understand what Cirque du Soleil has figured out about how to create a performance filled with wonder, it is useful to spend a minute thinking about the history of performance and the circus. We can only assume that humans have been performing for a long time. One can imagine cave dwellers telling jokes or playing their version of charades in preparation for a big hunt. We know of plays performed in ancient Greece, of Viking sagas acted out with great demonstrations of strength, of jesters in the royal courts whose livelihood and very lives depended on their ability to entertain and amuse the king, and of sailors in the sixteenth century passing the time at sea by singing and acting out songs about what they would find at their unknown destinations and what they left behind in the world they knew.

Then, of course, there is the circus, which originated in China and Rome about 2,500 years ago. The Chinese circus featured amazing feats of acrobatics, balance, and human contortion. The Roman circus had a somewhat different purpose with its chariot races, gladiator combat, theatrical performances, and animal sacrifices. The western circus and its use of three rings traces its beginning to Britain in about 1760. In those days, skilled riders did daring maneuvers on horseback within rings that defined the circumference at which horses could be ridden fast without falling over.

It is fun to think about the remarkable array of performances that people created before we even get to Shakespearean theatre, sym-

Think about the experience of being your customer from start to finish.

phonies, opera, the modern circus with its elephants, lions, high-wire acts, and people being shot from cannons, sporting events, motion pictures, Broadway musicals and rock concerts. And somehow parts of almost all of these have found their way into a Cirque du Soleil performance.

Business as a Performance

What makes a performance compelling is its ability to transport the audience to another place filled with wonder and possibilities. It appeals to our senses and our sense of what is special. We are confronted with something that is different than anything we have seen or experienced before, and the hope is that we will find it to be valuable. In a Cirque du Soleil performance, there are things to see everywhere: unusual characters; unusual costumes; a story that we can try to follow; stories in the story; music; fire; feats of great skill and daring; brute force; and sheer gracefulness.

Just like Cirque du Soleil, every company and organization produces a show that goes on every day. Each has a story that it is trying to tell the customers it chooses to serve. Each has actors playing big and small parts, a script, costumes, one or more sets, props, and an audience waiting to be engaged and thrilled. If the story isn't compelling, if the actors don't know their roles and how to work together or if the setting isn't right, your performance is quickly irrelevant. Try to think about all of the businesses and other organizations you know that really have their acts together and what they are doing right. Then think about their performances from start to finish.

Figure out what are the defining moments of your performance and how you can make them as remarkable as possible.

For example, the finest shopping centers and shopping districts in cities and many small towns use carefully orchestrated performances that are designed to attract shoppers and keep them interested, engaged and purchasing more—especially during the key holiday shopping seasons. The performance begins with the opening, typically at 10:00 AM, when all of the merchants have their shops in perfect order and are ready to greet the first guests. Throughout the course of the day, a set of activities and promotions seeks to engage patrons. These might include performers to entertain their children, product demonstrations to make customers more involved, smarter and different food options to satisfy the appetite, and special sales. The details of the performance change with the specifics of the season or holiday.

Each shop also has its own unique performance—some impressive and some missing the mark. These performances are a combination of the products or services they have for sale, the skill and level of engagement of the employees, the music, color, uniforms, and other elements designed to stir the senses.

Or think of the performance of an electrical parts supplier that begins early in the day when contractors arrive to pick up supplies for the jobs they are working on. The supplier needs to make sure that items are stocked and employees are knowledgeable about the options and quick at getting what everyone needs. They also need to have the latest and greatest products available in order to keep their customers up to date. They must be prepared to give a quick tutorial on how to install a part or on the most common challenges that other customers have faced. This coaching ability is an essential aspect of their performance. Their performance might continue by being easily accessible if a contractor calls from a job site with a question or needs something else. In that case, rapid delivery might appear in the show.

Consider an overnight delivery company that works to create a performance that is the actual embodiment of speed, discipline, and focus. They need to be prompt and efficient in picking up a parcel, understanding the specific requirements of a customer, explaining the options, and then getting the ball (or package) rolling. Their performance involves a number of handoffs from one performer to the next amid changing scenes and settings. At each change, they need to be skilled and coordinated in order to make sure the package arrives safely and on time at the other

Determine how to orchestrate the customer's entire experience with your organization with a sense of purpose and energy.

side of the continent or other side of the world. There another actor or actors will make sure the package gets to the final destination with speed and a smile.

To make these performances go off without a hitch requires the right planning, the right people, and the right practice. It also requires that we go beyond the usual in vital elements of our performances if we really want to be different in ways that matter to the customers we choose to serve. Arturo Toscanini, the great orchestra conductor, once remarked, "How you rehearse is how you perform." Practice is essential to making a performance compelling.

What Is Your Performance?

So what is your company or organization's performance and how is it different from that of Cirque du Soleil? A great way to understand this is to think about the experience of being your customer from start to finish.

- In what ways do you set the scene for delivering value?
- How does your show begin?
- How do you bring the customer or prospective customer into the performance?
- Who are the actors, how well are they trained, and what knowledge and tools do they bring to the show?
- How do they work together to seamlessly support each other, and how do they share information and make the right handoffs so the customer's needs are always met?
- How do they bring new ideas to each other and the customers?
- What "costumes" and "props" reinforce the experience you are trying to deliver?
- How do you create the opportunity to create the next performance for the customer?

- How does all of this carefully surround the products, services, and solutions that your company or organization has to offer?

But first, start with your story. What is the fundamental purpose that you bring to the customer? Is it to entertain them? To make them successful beyond measure? To enable them to do things they could never do without you and your offerings? Use your purpose as the focus of the performance you create and strive to put the customer at the center or at least, as they do at Cirque du Soleil, bring the customer into the show by breaking down the barriers that separate you from them. Then figure out what are the defining moments of your performance and how you can make them as remarkable as possible.

A great performance is unique and powerful, challenging our senses on many levels.

Obviously, the start of the customer experience is the first defining moment, and the end of each transaction is another. Depending on your business, there will be several along the way that you need to understand from the customer's perspective and seek to make as brilliant and captivating as possible.

Once you have figured it out, determine how to orchestrate the customer's entire experience with your organization with a sense of purpose and energy!

Take Your Own Journey

Now take your own journey. Great performances are everywhere and so are not-so-great ones. Your assignment is to take your team to a world-class performance of any kind you choose, although certain ones are likely to be a bit more insightful. It can be a leading ballet company or modern dance troupe, a musical or dramatic play, an orchestra concert or a virtuoso performance, or a sporting event featuring a team or an organization that is first rate. It can even be the circus. In fact, the circus—with its unique sense of creativity and drama—would be a great place to start, whether it is Cirque du Soleil, the Big Apple Circus, Ringling Brothers, or another circus.

If nothing interesting is coming to town and you are in a hurry to gain insight or you have a relatively small budget, you might start by simply buying a copy of "Alegria" or another performance of Cirque du Soleil on DVD and committing to watch it as a team. You might want to provide popcorn or other (healthy) snacks to help set the mood and, if possible, arrange to watch it on a large screen.

A great performance is unique and powerful, challenging our senses on many levels. It keeps us engaged and wondering what will happen next. It also gives us a much keener appreciation of the importance of everyone's role and the teamwork and collaboration required to make great things happen.

In case you haven't guessed already, I love the magic and genius of Cirque du Soleil and its amazing gift of creativity and daring. If they can reinvent something as great as the circus, there is no reason why you can't reinvent your business. It might be the key to the success of your customers and your organization.

chapter Eight

Your Wish Is My Command

The Big Idea:

We can win in business by solving practically any request no matter how difficult.

The Journey:

To spend a day with the chef concierge at one of the world's finest hotels...

Our companies and organizations are being tested by customers and potential customers every day. They test our offerings to make sure they live up to their reasonable and sometimes unreasonable expectations. They test our ability to support our offerings to make sure they are getting the most value out of what we say we deliver. They test our people's knowledge, responsiveness, enthusiasm, and commitment to serve them. They test us to see if we are able to keep bringing new ideas to them that make a difference. Sometimes they test us by asking for the impossible or the nearly impossible. So imagine what we could learn from people who make their living handling the requests of some of the world's most demanding people in one of the most demanding environments. Imagine spending a day with one of the most highly respected concierges in the world and his team at a remarkable five-star and five-diamond hotel. And don't be surprised if some of the problems or "opportunities" that he and his team get to solve catch you off guard.

New York City

Only five years old, the Ritz-Carlton on Central Park South has already established itself as one of the top hotels in the United States and was named one of the "world's best hotels in 2006" by *Travel + Leisure* magazine. It is a beautiful property with a great location right in the heart of New York City, directly across the street from Frederic Law Olmstead's and Calvert Vaux's amazing park. It is also a property that offers its guests impeccable service, some of the best-appointed rooms in the city, and some of the most spectacular views of Manhattan.

Like all Ritz-Carlton hotels, the highest standards of customer service are central to the value proposition. This service is a priority for every one of the hotel's employees, all 450 of them, who stand ready to serve at the drop of a hat. That's 1.6 employees per guest, a remarkably high number by any business standard. And every employee in the hotel is empowered to spend up to $2,000 to make a guest happy by addressing an issue that matters and correcting it.

With any request, the focus is the same: this guest and this inquiry matter more than anything in the world.

The hotel's guests are pretty special in their own right. They include royalty, heads of state, rock stars, sports stars, famous authors, business leaders, high-tech entrepreneurs, and a host of other celebrities. All come with their own unique needs and desires. With rooms costing anywhere from $800 to $12,000 per night, the hotel's guests expect to be treated well, and they expect their service and experience to be personalized.

Guests arrive by taxi, limousine, and occasionally horse-drawn carriage after a ride around Central Park. They enter a lobby of rich woods, beautiful freshly cut flowers, handsome and responsive people, and a feeling of great warmth. They also enter an environment of palpable affluence as people of means meet over a beverage, grab a bite of roasted beet and goat cheese salad, catch up on the latest news, stocks, or sports at the bar, or wait for a friend or colleague.

It's all about relationships and relating to people as individuals.

At the center of a great hotel is the Concierge Desk, a bustling hub of information, ideas, and soothing conversation. If a guest has a simple request, the staff will handle it with a smile and a quick call or a few keystrokes on the computer. If the request is more challenging, their collective creativity will be set in motion. With any request, the focus is the same: this guest and this inquiry matter more than anything in the world.

It was in this environment at the Ritz-Carlton that I had the pleasure of spending a day with Frederick Bigler, the chef concierge. Frederick has been at this property since it opened and has built an amazing team of nine concierges—each one probably capable of being the chef concierge at another high-end hotel. But here they form a remarkable team stationed either standing front and center or sitting in a veritable closet behind the concierge station. Their world is hopping with guests stopping by to make a request, guests calling from their rooms to get information or plan a night on the town, future guests calling or sending e-mails concerning their reservation, spouses of businesspeople calling to make arrangements for next month's visit to shop in New York, or personal assistants of corporate executives trying to work out the details for their boss's arrival or an important meeting. The phones and e-mails seem unending—all from people with significant demands and equally high expectations.

It turns out that being knowledgeable is often the most useful quality.

The Ritz-Carlton chain, even as one of the world's premier luxury brands, is itself in a state of change as it continues to meet the needs of the guests for whom it was designed and to adapt to the changing requirements of a new generation of affluent and successful visitors. While it is certainly not hip, the company recognizes the need to be more flexible. In the process, it is even changing the way its people communicate with guests from the traditional "It's my pleasure," a response I received to many of my requests during the day, to a more personalized touch based on a sense of who the guest is and what would appeal to them. This new tact makes a lot of sense but it requires more skill on the part of employees and that takes training, time, and practice.

Underneath it all is an amazing commitment to excellence in the quality of the hotel's product, its people, and the guest service that accompanies it. And don't think that the Ritz-Carlton doesn't have formidable competitors in the battle for hotel guests with a lot of money.

"Every guest needs to feel that they are important, their request is important, that we are working on it, and that it matters to us" was a common refrain I heard from Frederick and his colleagues. That philosophy includes the guests who aren't a total delight to work with.

So what kinds of requests do guests make?

First, there are the more common requests: getting last-minute theater tickets to a sold-out show or dinner reservations at one of the city's hottest restaurants like Per Se; having a stain removed before an important meeting; getting front row seats to tonight's Yankees game that starts in two hours; quickly putting together a new wardrobe for an executive whose luggage was lost and is heading to meetings in London in the evening—from shirts, pants, shoes that will be comfortable, underwear, and a new suitcase; making eight copies of a fax; arranging an after-hours tour of an exclusive gallery or a famous museum; making reservations for a performance at Lincoln Center eight months from now; finding a Brooklyn-born and raised tour guide who can give a former New Yorker a "memory lane" tour; getting a limo almost instantly; returning shirts to Bergdorf Goodman; locating hard-to-find electronics that are available only in Hong Kong and having them in New York in 24 hours; picking up five pairs of shoes at Barney's for the wife

Every time you meet people, treat them well.

of a visiting head of state; and planning a romantic weekend, an engagement party, or an adventure in the city.

All are straightforward requests for a skilled concierge. And all are part of the expectations of customers who are used to getting everything they ask for and who are, for the most part, very reasonable when they are treated well.

What are the more unusual or challenging requests that a concierge might receive?

A visiting prime minister asked for Orville Redenbacher's Caramel Popcorn which, as it turned out, was not available in any store in New York City. After calls to likely places failed, Frederick decided to call the company's corporate headquarters. There he found out that the closest location was a gourmet store in the suburbs. A car was dispatched to buy the treat and the customer's wish was fulfilled. The lesson here was to go straight to the source.

One time a successful entrepreneur wanted to have a special weekend celebration for his wife's fortieth birthday. To meet this request, Frederick created a "Charlie's Angels" weekend adventure for her and two of her closest friends. Every morning he placed under each of their room doors a cassette that provided whispered instructions on a day filled with nonstop shopping, dining, sightseeing, and entertainment adventures planned for their enjoyment. One day included buying 1960s clothes at a trendy retro shop, getting 1960s hairstyles, and seeing the play "Hairspray" from great seats. It was a huge hit. The lesson here was to take a fresh look at every request, then know where to find things that make a difference.

These skills are not only for serving the pleasures of the rich. They can also be used to teach an important lesson. When the CEO of a Fortune 500 corporation asked for special gift ideas for his child who had everything, Frederick thought about the gift of giving and created a unique hotel package to meet this difficult request. The package was a "philanthropy" weekend, and here are the details published by the hotel:

The Philanthropy and Tea Package

Rate: *From $730 USD per night*

For the child who has everything, we opt for the gift of giving. We will have a car take them to FAO Schwartz where they can hand-select toys for underprivileged children in New York City. Your child will have the choice of hand delivering each gift or having us deliver the toys while you both enjoy afternoon tea in the Star Lounge. To reward your child for all of his or her hard work, we will deliver a plate of cookies and milk to your room before bedtime and will have thank-you notes written to them.

- *Based upon availability, luxurious accommodations for two in a Park View Room or Park View Suite*
- *Two night minimum stay*
- *Valid for a Friday, Saturday, or Sunday night stay only*
- *Shopping trip to FAO Schwartz arranged by our Concierge*
- *Afternoon tea for two in the Star Lounge*
- *Cookies and milk at turndown*

There are many other examples, such as finding an armored vehicle to transport the wives of the Sultan of Brunei on a shopping trip when they expressed concern about their safety, finding a veterinarian to make a house call at the hotel for a rock star's injured puppy, or training 800 volunteers in the art of the concierge so they could more effectively staff hotel support desks for delegates to the Republican National Convention.

It's all in a day's work.

According to Frederick, the most essential skills for success as a concierge are talent, personality, a genuine desire to care for customers, professional service skill, and an ability to think outside the box everyday. It's all about relationships and relating to people as individuals—"keeping it real for them." It's also about having an amazing network and continuing to develop that network of restaurant owners, theater managers, business managers, museum directors, store owners and managers, other concierges, and anyone who might need to be called on to address a guest's request. There is an international association of the world's leading concierges, and even though the hotels are competitors they work together as colleagues to help each other meet the needs of guests.

It turns out that being knowledgeable is often the most useful quality. Who's dating a particular maitre d'? Who knows someone who might know someone at a particular art gallery or club? So building your network, reading, and hanging out everywhere (which is tough in a city as big as New York) are essential. Every time you meet people, treat them well. As Frederick says, "What you put out comes back to you in a big way. [You create] friendships where you may not see them often but can pick up right where you left off."

> **Start by creating a culture of responsiveness and collaboration in which all of us work as a team to solve customer problems.**

Who would be drawn to life as a concierge? The cast here sheds an interesting light on this career choice as it includes an opera singer, a former dancer, and an aspiring teacher. But most importantly it is people who like people and want to see them happy, people who like to make things happen for other people, people who are passionate about solving problems and creating opportunities.

Customer Requests Matter

The word "concierge" seems overused today. Type it in a Google search, and you will be amazed at the people and organizations calling themselves concierges and the variety of settings in which the idea, or some facsimile of it, is being used. But that shouldn't detract from the compelling power of this idea as it relates to companies and organizations that must, to succeed, spend a good deal of time solving customer requests.

Customer requests matter. They certainly matter to them, and they should matter to us. But if we aren't organized or skilled enough to respond to them effectively, they have the potential to become one of our greatest nightmares. Yet it doesn't have to be that way. We can start by creating **Make usable all of the insight, experiences, and customer interactions that people have.** a culture of responsiveness and collaboration in which all of us work as a team to solve customer problems. The key is to quickly let the customer know that we understand the request, that it really matters to us, and that our organization is giving it our undivided attention. Then behind the scenes we can work together to figure it out.

Imagine if your help desk actually functioned like the concierge desk at the Ritz-Carlton, where talented people quickly handle the routine requests and think creatively about the more unusual inquiries. You would have a chance to blow your competition away.

What if everyone in your organization acted liked a skilled concierge, eager to figure out a creative way to make a difference in the lives of the customers you choose to serve? What if they took ownership for the customer's issue and committed that it mattered to them and they would do whatever it took to try to solve it? What if they were connected to each other and the world around them? And what if companies and organizations did a better job of listening to the people at the front lines of customer service who see the customer's joys and frustrations firsthand?

Networks and knowledge management are essential. We can dramatically improve our ability to respond to any customer request if we can somehow harness the information on all the customer requests we have handled with skill before. This could mean having an elaborate system in place that records each request in detail and the way it was addressed. Or we could rely on sharing knowledge in a less formal way. A skilled team of concierges can succeed with a good Rolodex, some basic notes, and a commitment to sharing information with each other. But the bigger and more complex our organizations are, the greater likelihood that some systematic response is essential if we are going to capture and make usable all of the insight, experiences, and customer interactions that people have.

As for basic rules, here's Frederick's list of the most essential ones:

- Acknowledge everyone and make eye contact with everyone.
- Return every call.
- Give every customer the clear sense that their request really matters and that you will try your best to make it happen. Then, even if you can't make it happen, they will appreciate the effort you put into it.
- Understand that the world of customers and requests is always changing by making your interactions personal and real.
- Build the strongest possible network and continue to develop and strengthen your relationships in it.

- Give back to the world—everyone you work with and everyone who needs your help—and it will come back to you. Set an example by being thoughtful and generous.

How Do You Handle Requests?

So how do you and your company or organization handle questions and requests? What kinds of requests do your customers make? Just like the guests at the Ritz-Carlton, they probably fall into two categories—relatively common and a bit more unusual. And just like the concierge staff at the Ritz-Carlton, you and your colleagues can be prepared to quickly handle the common ones. The others will require a bit more creativity.

You can handle the tough ones by building your own internal and external networks to quickly track down the best response. To do this, you will have to create a culture of collaboration focused squarely on the customers you choose to serve. Imagine that all of your people are connected in some way and that they have access to essential information about each other's knowledge, expertise, and

Understand that the world of customers and requests is always changing by making your interactions personal and real.

connections. Then imagine that you could continually update this information as you develop more experience handling common and challenging requests. You might also begin to see the logic in periodically bringing everyone together to share stories about their finest moments of creative problem-solving that made a real difference for your customers. Then your organization would be in a powerful position to respond to customers.

Take Your Own Journey

Now take your own journey. Your assignment on this field trip should be a lot of fun because you now have a chance to live (or at least pretend to live) like the people we all read about in magazines. You know, they're the ones who wear expensive clothes, drive expensive cars, stay at fancy hotels, and jet-set to remote islands where they are pampered beyond belief and then have messy public divorces. But seriously, now is your chance to see how the finest service providers deliver the finest service. And there is no reason why you and your colleagues shouldn't deserve the same treatment.

The World of High-End Products and Services.

Head off to the most fashionable shopping district in your community. There you'll find retailers who sell products and services that cater to people willing to spend a lot of money for more personal attention and greater value, or at least greater perceived value. Surely these merchants—who charge a premium for their clothes, accessories, fine foods, beverages, dining experiences, personal grooming, travel arrangements, and so on—are willing to go above and beyond the call of duty to meet the unique needs of their customers. Pick four or five stores to visit, explore, and learn from. They can be one-of-a-kind local businesses or branches of a national or international company. Now go in and have a look around. Spend some time talking with the folks who work there and maybe some of the customers. Try to figure out what goes on in these shops, what sets them apart

Create a culture of collaboration focused squarely on the customers you choose to serve.

from other merchants selling similar types of products and services, and how they offer and deliver satisfaction.

An old adage states, "It is better to be rich and healthy than sick and poor," and I guess it applies equally well to customers. Those businesses that cater to people of means, for whom budget is not a huge issue, are pretty lucky, assuming, of course, that they can deliver compelling value. But even if our customers' resources are a bit more constrained, the ability to handle any request could be part of a formula for winning in our markets and for creating a culture of amazing responsiveness.

The ability to handle any request could be part of a formula for winning in our markets and for creating a culture of amazing responsiveness.

In case you haven't guessed already, I left my day with Frederick Bigler and his team of problem-solving geniuses at the Ritz-Carlton Hotel with an even stronger sense that we could all be more successful if we thought and acted like a world-class concierge. Not that I can afford to stay at the Ritz-Carlton on Central Park South. But, after all, our customers would like to believe that their requests matter and that we really care.

Chapter Nine

When Every Second Counts

The Big Idea:

We can win in business by being ready, available, and brilliant 24/7.

The Journey:

To a shock trauma center where lifesaving decisions are made every minute . . .

The era of the 9:00 to 5:00 or even 8:00 to 6:00 business day is a thing of the past. It has been replaced by a fast-paced, turbocharged, hyper-competitive global economy in which more and more customers are living and working around the clock. And they expect the companies and organizations that serve them to do the same, not simply by giving lip service to the notion of "24/7" but by being ready to deliver value at a moment's notice.

Yet most firms and organizations do little more than merely talk about the notion of being ready, willing, and brilliant around the clock. But imagine that you no longer had a choice. Then imagine what you would have to do if your customer's success really hangs in the balance. What if your failure to be there with just the right skill or knowledge at any moment of the day could influence their very life or at least their livelihood? Some people actually choose to live in this world because it is the only way to make a compelling difference in the lives of those they serve. So let's spend a day with the team at the world's leading shock trauma center to find out what they do when life really does hang in the balance every minute, 24/7, 365 days a year.

Baltimore, Maryland

It's 2:00 AM. The harsh sound of an ambulance interrupts the night as it races to the R. Adams Cowley Shock Trauma Center at the University of Maryland Medical Center in the heart of downtown Baltimore. Inside the ambulance, emergency medical personnel are struggling to save the life of a young man who was shot several times as he stood outside of a popular nightclub. They are also calling the hospital with their best assessment of his condition so its entire team can be prepared to save his life. I could have said "to try" to save his life, but that is not the mission of this remarkable trauma center and the overall system that supports it. This place exists to save his life no matter how critically injured he is. Its success rate is impressive: last year 97 percent of 7,700 admissions survived, many of whom were on the edge of death.

Two phones on the wall next to the nurses' station serve as a command post. The yellow phone brings calls from the first responders in the field who quickly alert the center that they have someone to bring in and provide an initial assessment of what has happened and their condition. A white phone provides updates of each patient's status en route to the center and what the personnel in the ambulance or the medevac helicopter are doing to treat them.

Six minutes later, the ambulance arrives at the emergency room door where a critical care nurse and two medical technicians are waiting. From there they will race the patient to the second-floor trauma resuscitation unit as they continue to assess his condition in order to determine the skills, technology, and treatment that will be required to reverse the injuries he has sustained. If he is still conscious and able to respond, the nurse will ask some basic questions along the way: "What's your name?" "What happened?" "What's bothering you?" Each question intended to help gauge the extent of his injuries and trauma and the appropriate next steps in his care.

In a more important and compelling sense, every admission to this unique hospital is met by the entire hospital's team of nurses, technicians, and physicians. No one who is needed is on call. At any moment of any day, world-class professionals in every single specialty are on site at the hospital, all ready to head to the second floor. Each stands ready at a moment's notice to bring to bear whatever specialized expertise is required to save a life.

They are supported by the latest and most accessible technology available. Within the self-contained world of the trauma resuscitation unit are 12 identical assessment bays, six identical operating units, and all of the essential diagnostic equipment and services that would be needed to treat any patient. This includes the Statscan machine that can make a detailed total body scan in 13 seconds, enabling the medical team to pinpoint the exact location of any bullets or fractures. It also includes the latest X-ray equipment, CT scanner, angiogram equipment, ventilators, its own supply of all blood types, and a direct connection to the lab which can complete diagnostic work within five minutes. As one nurse put it, "It's a lot like a spaceship in here—anything we need for any case is literally within 100 feet of any patient."

During the next twenty-four hours, the hospital staff will see twenty-five new patients. On the day I visited the center, this included the victim of a high-speed car crash and rollover, a man with three stab wounds in the back, someone with a severe spinal cord injury from a fall, a person with multiple broken bones from a fall, and a woman who was 27 weeks pregnant who had been kicked in the stomach by a horse.

While the case we began with came by ambulance from the too often dangerous streets of the city, we could have just as easily followed a medevac helicopter as it sped from the scene of a highway accident, poisoning, or construction or boating accident to the helipad on the center's roof. Again the patient would have been met by the same team and rushed within the same two minutes to the second-floor

Most firms and organizations do little more than provide lip service to the notion of being ready, willing, and brilliant around the clock.

trauma resuscitation unit. About 60 percent of the center's patients come as a result of motor vehicle accidents, 25 percent

as a result of interpersonal violence, and most of the remaining
15 percent as a result of industrial or recreational accidents.

The fact that they are all rushed here and then to treatment
is vital to this story—the history of the R. Adams Cowley Shock
Trauma Center, its remarkable success, and the modern practice
of trauma care.

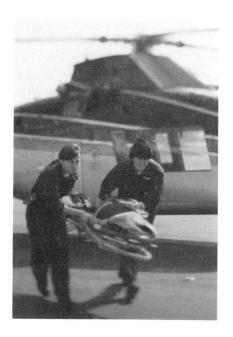

The Golden Hour

Central to this place, and now to the world of trauma medicine,
is the concept of the "golden hour," the sixty-minute window
after people are critically injured when what happens will determine whether they survive and what the quality of their lives
will be. They might live for many days after their injury, but in
the absence of the right care they will not make it. This concept,
pioneered by Dr. R. Adams Cowley, the hospital's founder and
a visionary in the field of trauma care, is central to everything

that goes on here. That includes the design of the hospital, the makeup and training of its staff, and the overall statewide emergency medical system that supports it. Mean time from accident to the center by helicopter is only 18 minutes.

The "golden hour" has never been scientifically proven, but it is, according to Dr. Thomas Scalea, the center's physician-in-chief, "absolute as a concept" and "the guiding principle" in the practice of trauma care. It could, in reality, be six minutes, sixty minutes, or even ninety minutes, depending on what has happened to a particular person and the extent of their injuries and trauma, but it is the critical window in which the right lifesaving treatment must occur.

Dr. Scalea leads the center with remarkable energy and passion for saving lives and an infectious ability to convince you that practically anything is possible. To prove this, he describes the most recent amazing cases in which heroic effort by people at every step of the process combined with a willingness to take informed risk and literally "invent new procedures on the fly" brought patients back from the brink of death.

Moving over to his computer, he pulls up a presentation on the case of a sixteen-year-old female who sustained a traumatic brain injury after being thrown from a moving golf cart. After initial surgery, the patient's condition became increasingly complicated. With few good options available, the center's team made the decision to remove part of her skull in order to relieve the pressure on her brain and to place her in a completely upright position on a tilting table to perform the rest of her surgery—both dramatic innovations in the field of trauma care. Soon after, the young

Each stands ready at a moment's notice to bring to bear whatever specialized expertise is required to save a life.

woman's condition stabilized, and she was discharged to a traumatic brain injury rehabilitation facility. Within three months, she returned to her normal routine and was recently accepted into the freshman class at one of America's leading (and most competitive) private universities.

Heroic effort by people at every step of the process combined with a willingness to take informed risk and literally "invent new procedures on the fly" brought patients back from the brink of death.

At the annual dinner given to honor the R. Adams Cowley Shock Trauma Center and the system's people for their heroic efforts, this case and others like it were presented, and everyone who touched the lives of the patients was asked to come onstage. For each case, roughly sixty people came up to be acknowledged for their roles in avoiding death.

Dr. Scalea attributes the center's amazing success to the right combination of people, the right system that starts in the field, cutting-edge insight and technology, a willingness to do whatever it takes, and the shared belief—expressed by everyone I spoke with—that they can save every single patient. "Our commitment is that we will not let them die" was a constant refrain. That is the message they give to every patient and every family. Tied to this is a remarkable consistency of nursing and physician/specialist care at any minute of any day. In their world, you are only as good as your weakest day or your weakest moment, so you had better commit to being brilliant all the time. The notion of 24/7 even applies to chaplains who are available around the clock, a suggestion made by the nursing staff in response to the needs of patients' families.

But how do you create a culture that can deliver on such a compelling promise even with the best people and the best system in place? According to Dr. Scalea, it is a relatively simple equation:

First, "you have to inspire genius from the top down." Unlike many leaders, Dr. Scalea is visible and engaged all the time. He has regularly worked 100-hour weeks since he came to the center ten years ago, and last year he performed 585 operative cases. He makes it clear that he is always available if someone needs him. Take the case of the pregnant woman kicked in the stomach by a horse. The challenge was to save the mother and the baby. The doctor handling the case wanted another opinion and called Dr. Scalea at 10:30 PM to exchange ideas. Dr. Scalea then called two other specialists to get their insight before calling the physician back to discuss the case further. At the end of their conversation, he asked if he should come in. By now the physician felt comfortable enough to handle the case.

You are only as good as your weakest day or your weakest moment, so you had better commit to being brilliant all the time.

Talking with nurses, physicians, technicians, and other staff at the hospital confirms that his sense of purpose and possibility is contagious. "We don't give up" was a theme echoed in every department, along with the shared focused on the reward of saving a life. There is a unique spirit of teamwork and collaboration here that runs counter to notions many of us have about the hierarchy of modern medicine and doctor-centric depictions of nurses and support staff on popular television shows. One nurse who had been at the center for almost 30 years told me, "Dr. Cowley used to tell all the doctors that they had to make sure to take care of the nurses, and Dr. Scalea is equally committed to this ideal."

Second, "you have to sell the dream that they are doing a great thing." Fortunately, it is not hard to make the connection in a place like this. People want to work at the center and be part of its lifesaving mission. And they don't want to let each other down. But you still have to give people the confidence in their own ability to be successful. And you have to allow them to take ownership of the problems they face. It is this sense of support and ownership that drives people's desire to solve problems and make great things happen.

Third, "you have to believe you can do the impossible." The people who arrive at the center are badly broken, and yet there is a compelling belief that everyone can be saved. But even with advances in both technology and our understanding of human physiology, it isn't an easy task. Yet day after day, the hospital's team figures out how to save someone who probably has no chance to still be alive. These cases serve to show people the power they have as a team to make a difference, which in turn seems to get them up for any challenge. Even the times when a patient dies seem to strengthen the team's resolve to do whatever it takes to save the next life.

When asked what's next in their efforts to save lives, Dr. Scalea smiles and says that they are hoping someday soon to start freezing people who are close to death so they can stop their hearts and the process of trauma, fix their injuries, and then

Inspire genius from the top down.

rewarm them. He cites promising studies in animals as a reason for optimism about the potential to save some patients who would die otherwise. "How's that," he suggests, "for inspiring greatness!"

The Whole System Matters

I have mentioned that the system supporting the center is vital to its success, and it is important to make this a bit clearer. In a world driven by the "golden hour," there is no time to waste. Part of Dr. Cowley's vision was a statewide emergency medical system that could quickly bring any critically injured patient to the care that was essential to save his or her life. This meant having the right combination of facilities across the state and a transport system that could bring the most critically injured people to the highest level of care in time to increase their likelihood of survival. It also meant being able to provide a higher level of expertise and care during transport. As it turned out, Maryland was the perfect place to do this with its relatively small geography and infrastructure of hospitals and medical facilities.

Throughout the state there are nine adult and two pediatric trauma centers (one of which is actually the Children's National Medical Center in Washington, D.C.) and a network of specialty referral centers that treat burns, hand injuries, and eye trauma. Taken together, these centers provide a focused and organized network of essential skills and resources in a system designed to ensure that injured patients are treated at the best place to meet their needs. At the heart of these is R. Adams Cowley, the only dedicated shock trauma hospital in the United States and, by most accounts, the "Mecca" of trauma care. It is a place where medical professionals from all around the world and the front lines of military combat come to learn and train.

Give people the confidence in their own ability to be successful.

It is also a place that has been made accessible to practically anyone in the state through a sophisticated helicopter transport system that operates from eight strategically located bases across Maryland. From these locations, world-class emergency medical personnel can quickly get to the scene of an accident and then on to the center with the skills to perform life-sustaining procedures such as tracheotomies in flight.

The right system, design, vision, expertise, commitment to collaboration in saving lives, and passion for doing the impossible—all delivered at any moment of any day. These are the compelling ingredients that unlock the genius in this place and all of its people.

Being Brilliant 24/7 Matters

One of the hottest phrases in business today is "24/7." Recognizing that we are in a very competitive and very global economy, there is growing awareness that we need to be available around the clock to meet customer needs. But "24/7" has become so much jargon. Every company seems to use it in some way. It is hip to be "24/7" and part, it seems, of the new minimum daily requirement for customer service. But how many companies and organizations really are? How many can bring to bear the most essential knowledge, expertise, and ability at any moment of the day no matter when the "ambulance" arrives?

It is in some way fitting to use an example from healthcare to talk about what it means to be available and brilliant all the time (though I realize that our overall healthcare system and the field of emergency medicine, in particular, are facing great challenges today—with costs seemingly spiraling out of control and many high-profile cases of mistakes in treatment being reported in leading publications). The University of Maryland R. Adams Cowley Shock Trauma Center is unique. It is actually "profitable" (in nonprofit organization terms), thanks to receiving dedicated funding from the state, and able to attract some of the best and most highly motivated staff for its lifesaving work. But I do believe that anywhere in the United States or the world the best institutions and most skilled and motivated nurses, doctors, and other staff understand the importance of being brilliant 24/7 when it matters.

As companies we have started to use many phrases from healthcare. We have customer "care" systems that are designed, one might presume, to really care about the customers and their needs. We have customer "care" professionals who are trained, one might also presume, to "remedy" customer concerns. We even talk about "triaging" customers, not unlike the triage nurse at the emergency room so that our limited resources can be applied, apparently, to the most valuable or desperate ones. For while it would be great to provide brilliant "care" to every customer, economics suggest that most companies or organizations focus on the biggest or best. But do we really care about our customers? And do we have the systems, skills, and passion in place to make a compelling difference in their lives?

Being brilliant 24/7 means being organized to deliver value to the customer at all times and knowing what to do under any circumstances. It means having the right people with the right training, motivation, and commitment to serve the customers. It means being brilliant at communicating with each other, regularly assessing customer needs, and mastering the essential handoffs that will determine if the customer gets the right expertise (or care) at precisely the right time. While most of us aren't dealing with life and death situations, we should behave as though they are if we want to be far better than our competitors.

Show people the power they have as a team to make a difference, which in turn seems to get them up for any challenge.

Remember the insight from Frederick Bigler at the Ritz Carlton—make every guest know that their request matters to you and that it is receiving your complete attention. At the moment when we are serving a customer they are the most important person in our world. At the Shock Trauma Center this is definitely the case whether the patient is a child who was critically injured in a car accident or a convicted felon who was stabbed in prison.

Why is 24/7 So Difficult for the Rest of Us?

So if everyday geniuses at the R. Adams Cowley Shock Trauma Center can save people 24/7, why can't most companies solve relatively simple customer requests at any time of the day or night? To understand this, let me take you on my final call to Dell "On Call," the 24/7 technical support center for this leading computer company's customers. It began with the following automated message:

"Thank you for calling Dell On Call, Dell's help desk telephone support service for technology issues not covered by your Dell hardware warranty. Please have your Dell On Call order number ready for the next available technician. Please note that we will not be able to provide support without a valid order number."

That seemed like a reasonable start. In order to improve their efficiency and help me to solve my issue, I needed to be an appropriate customer with an appropriate issue and a valid order number. So far so good. This was the right contest, and I had a chance to win. But how long would it take to be served? As if they were reading my mind, the following message answered back:

"Please be advised that the wait is more than five minutes."

Given that I had a pressing problem which was either software, middleware, the menace of spyware, or some other evil "ware" of the non-hard variety that had decided to possess my computer at 6:45 PM eastern standard time, I was willing to stick it out. Surely "more than five minutes" would be only seven or eight minutes by my quick calculation. After all, this was Dell Corporation, an amazing business success story and until last year the acknowledged leader in personal computers. So I turned on the speaker phone and went about my business, or as much of my business as possible given the pathetic state of my PC. And the messages kept coming:

"Due to overwhelming demand we are currently experiencing high call volume. Please remain on the line for the next available technician."

You mean higher call volume than a world-class company had planned on? Or higher call volume than they had staffed for? Or some other variation of higher call volume that had created a serious mismatch between the needs of customers and the resources the company was willing to assign to address those needs?

Then a moment later, the following message:

"Did you know that Dell On Call is available twenty-four hours a day, seven days a week?" the pleasant automated voice asked me.

"I assumed it was," I replied back to the void on the other end of the line. In fact, I assumed it was available right now, which is the reason I called. Don't we all assume that 24/7 help desks are available 24/7? And their message simply confirmed that they had a somewhat different notion of what "twenty-four hours a day, seven days a week" actually meant.

"Please have your order number ready for the next available technician." And I was set with that one too. The minute their person picked up the phone I was ready, in my nicest voice, to slowly articulate Order Number 562345738, a number that I had memorized in the din between their canned messages. In fact, I was ready and willing to give them any information they wanted— short of compromising my

Being brilliant 24/7 means being organized to deliver value to the customer at all times and knowing what to do under any circumstances.

very identity—in exchange for someone helping me to get this sick puppy up and running again.

Then another important announcement:

"Dell On Call incidents can now be purchased online. If you would like to purchase additional incidents, please visit us online at www.dell.com/fmb/dell on call."

"Now that's a great offer," I replied. I was having so much fun on this call that I could only imagine the sheer joy of buying an incident multi-pack and spending as much of my time as possible on hold waiting for their technician.

Fortunately these messages continued to cycle over and over again for the forty-two minutes and fifty seconds that I waited for a technician. I say fortunately because there were moments during the call when I actually questioned whether Dell and its employees really cared about me. As we all know, customers like to be cared about. It is one of the subliminal reasons why we do business with companies and organizations. And I guess that Dell understood this and was trying to use this one-way automated dialogue to keep reminding me and the countless others around the globe who were also on the line just in case we never got help.

> **Customers like to be cared about. It is one of the subliminal reasons why we do business with companies and organizations.**

At 7:28 PM I decided to hang up and end the conversation with my automated friend at Dell. I was a bit sad that this relationship hadn't worked out as planned. But after calling a local computer consultant to help solve the problem, our small company decided to switch its business to another vendor—a decision we made based on a careful review of relatively comparable products and the hope that their service would be better than the low bar that Dell had set. I guess we were looking for someone who had roughly the same understanding of what 24/7 should mean.

Some people get it right, like the team at BNA Software, a leading producer of software products and support services for tax and accounting professionals. Their help desk, staffed by tax and accounting professionals, is really designed to be a knowledge center through which experts provide detailed guidance to customers on not only the technical aspects of the products but also how to use them most effectively. Their real purpose is to understand the world of the customer and help each to unlock value in their offerings that improves performance. Their system, staffing, and commitment are designed to quickly respond and then resolve customer issues.

How Brilliant Are You 24/7?

So what about you and your company or organization? Do you understand the evolving importance of being ready, willing, and skillful 24/7? Do you know enough about the customer to support their success at any moment of the day? And do you have the system, skill, and commitment to be there at the customer's time of need?

Most of us don't get the chance to save lives. But that doesn't mean we aren't doing things that matter. Our customers have needs that are essential to their success and, for many, their ultimate viability as companies and organizations. That should be enough of a motivator to get us to deliver compelling value whenever they need it. Now the challenge is to put in place the systems, people, skills, and commitment to collaboration essential to meeting their needs.

Commit to figuring out when 24/7 matters, or could matter, for the customers you choose to serve. Then figure out how to be different and brilliant in meeting their time-sensitive needs. You can start by making sure you are there for them in a way that shows real responsiveness and competence at their basic requirements.

Then think about how to connect all your people and knowledge so that you can deliver the right solution at any time. You might even think about how to use the Internet as part of the equation. But try to remember

> **Think about how to connect all your people and knowledge so that you can deliver the right solution at any time.**

that real humans who actually care about the customer and are willing to take ownership of the customer's problem are your most important weapon. They alone can demonstrate that they won't leave the customer until the problem is addressed (i.e., that they "won't let them die").

Take Your Own Journey

Now take your own journey. While I can't say that examples of true "24/7" brilliance are everywhere, I do know that more and more companies and organizations are seeing the importance of delivering value at any moment of the day. Whether they are being as successful as they could is a question you can explore.

So here are some ideas for getting you going . . .

Cast a Wide Net.

Head out into the world around you with your eyes wide open to any place where 24/7 seems to matter. Visit an all-night service center such as Kinko's at 2:00 AM, or a twenty-four-hour grocery store at 4:00 AM, or a popular all-night diner to see what happens in the hours when only the most desperate people are customers. If the businesses are doing a great job, try to figure out their secret recipe for making the clock irrelevant.

Then Look for Brilliant Product Support.

You might want to start by doing a bit of informal research with colleagues, friends. and customers to get their ideas on companies that provide great support. Then make a few calls at odd hours, even if you don't use their products, to see what type of response you get. You might even try to make your next plane reservations at 1:00 AM just to see what happens. With a bit of luck or through thoughtful design, you might end up having a great experience with shorter phone queues and someone who is really excited to meet a customer's needs.

I left the R. Adams Cowley Shock Trauma Center with a very different notion of what it means to be brilliant or geniuses 24/7 and what is possible when people are inspired to believe that together they can do the impossible.

chapter Ten

Fastest

The Big Idea:
We can win in business by being fast, but only when speed matters.

The Journey:
To the savanna of Tanzania and the remarkable world of the fastest creature on land ...

Speed matters. As customers, we want things quickly or even instantly. We buy faster cars, upgrade to higher-speed Internet connections, use same-day cleaners, and wait at the door for the fastest pizza delivery. We want vendors who can serve us quickly and get us the right product or replacement part overnight. We expect service to happen when we want it and are frustrated when it cannot. We see lines, queues, and waiting as the bane of our existence. We curse at long lines and robotic phone voices intended to prolong our suffering until the company on the other end can get its act together. "I'll wait," is our common refrain—but only because we believe we have no choice.

As companies, we strive to be faster as though that will be the key to our success. For some "do it faster" has become the new mantra based on the assumption that speed will win over customers. But have we mistaken an unconditional belief in speed for the need to be fast at only the most critical times in the lives of those we serve? And if we really want to be fast at the right times, should we turn to nature for our inspiration? Perhaps cheetahs, beautiful and remarkable animals designed for speed, will give us some clues. So imagine what we could learn by taking a journey to the unforgiving landscape of east Africa to see some of these amazing creatures who have to be fast when it matters.

Tanzania, East Africa

It's early in the morning on the savanna of Tanzania, and a lone female cheetah is quietly searching for prey. Sitting atop a termite hill, she surveys the landscape, hoping to spot a gazelle, impala, or small antelope. It turns out that seeing prey is not a problem. Cheetahs can see up to one and a quarter miles away. This incredible vision is one of the amazing gifts she will need if she and her cubs are going to eat today. The big challenge is being close enough when the actual hunt begins. To do this, she must be within about 300 feet to have a chance—even with her blazing speed. Though it is best if she can stalk her prey until it is within thirty to 100 feet. This distance provides a bit more room for error.

Suddenly an opportunity presents itself. An antelope is within range. The chase will last for maybe twenty seconds. With unmatched acceleration, the cheetah races after the startled animal and quickly knocks it over by striking its rear. She then sinks her teeth into the underside of the antelope's throat to cut off its air supply. In a matter of seconds, the antelope is dead. This is a good day. Cheetahs catch their prey only about half of the time. Imagine going to the grocery store and finding food only on every other visit.

Cheetahs, among the world's most beautiful and remarkable cats, are the fastest land mammals, capable of speeds approaching 70 miles per hour. They are also one of the few animal species in which males and females are the same size and reach the same speed. At their top speed, it looks as if they are literally flying through the air. The only animal that comes close is the gazelle, one of the cheetah's favorite prey, whose top speed is just under 60 miles per hour, which at least gives the gazelle a chance of survival.

Cheetahs are designed for speed, which is a very good thing. Without speed, they would have a lot of trouble staying alive. Their world is harsh and filled with many predators such as lions and hyenas that are much bigger and/or stronger than they are. Cheetahs quickly grow into their speed out of necessity. By the age of six months, a time when human babies are just figuring out how to crawl, a cheetah cub can go fast enough to avoid most danger, though that doesn't mean the cub could survive on its own. The cub will stay with its mother, to the extent that she survives, until it is about eighteen months old when she has taught it enough about hunting, avoiding predators, and basic survival to make its own way in the world. (If the mother dies before this time, the cubs are unlikely to survive.) Then for another six months, they will stay together as a sibling group until the females leave. Interestingly, the male cheetahs will often remain together for their entire lives.

Speed matters. As customers, we want things quickly or even instantly.

Cheetahs are small by big cat standards. The average adult weighs somewhere between 110 and 135 pounds. Compare this with an adult male lion that can weigh as much as 500 pounds. Cheetahs are not very powerful by big cat standards. Unlike lions and tigers, which are extremely strong and can overpower their enemies and their prey, cheetahs must rely on speed in order to survive.

Cheetahs are also relatively gentle by big cat standards. Unlike most big cats and many of the other animals in their world, cheetahs are not inclined to fight—not even among themselves. (This is another admirable cheetah trait that I've been trying to pass along to our three children.) Because of this, they often fall victim to having other animals steal their food, eat their young, or even eat them.

So imagine that you are one of the smallest and gentlest kids in a school full of bullies. In the absence of being able to fight or talk your way out of any situation, you'd better be able to run very fast.

Think of a cheetah as a cat that has been modified by nature to move very quickly:

- The most striking feature of the cheetah is its long legs which enable it to make exceedingly long strides. Their legs are much longer proportionally than the legs of any other cats.
- They also have a springy backbone that can be arched and stretched to lengthen their stride. At full speed, a cheetah's stride is about 20 feet long but has been measured as long as 32 feet.
- Cheetahs are very slender which helps them go faster.
- They have a smaller head for less wind resistance.
- They are amazingly muscular, with almost half of their muscle mass in their backs.
- They have a long tail that stabilizes them and helps them to balance when going fast and making quick changes in direction.
- They have long, semi-retractable claws and rough foot pads—much more like a dog's than a cat's—that allow them to grip the ground for control. In fact, their paws provide an excellent model for how to make a sure-footed running shoe or maybe even a better snow tire.

They have some other more subtle design features that help to increase their speed and ability to hunt. These include an enlarged heart, increased lung capacity, and wide nostrils. They also have high-set eyes to improve their range of vision and black "tear marks" running from the inner corner of their eyes to the mouth which help keep the sun out of their eyes during a chase.

This ability to accelerate matters when you are relatively small and can only go fast for a limited amount of time.

But their most amazing feature is their acceleration. Cheetahs can go from a standing start to 45 miles per hour in two seconds. Compare that with the acceleration of some expensive cars, and you're likely to wonder if the car owners got their money's worth:

Relative Acceleration of Cheetahs and High-Performance Cars			
	Miles per Hour	**Time**	**Cost**
Dodge Viper SRT10	0 – 60 mph	4.2 sec	$ 91,990
Chevrolet Corvette Z06	0 – 60 mph	4.3 sec	$ 76,730
Porsche 911 Carrera S	0 – 60 mph	4.4 sec	$ 87,520
Cheetah	0 – 45 mph	2.0 sec	Priceless

*Source: Car information from *Consumer Reports*,
"Supercar Test" (September 2006).

This ability to accelerate matters when you are relatively small and can only go fast for a limited amount of time. A cheetah's range at high speed is only about 300 to 500 meters. After this distance, they have to slow down. So being close enough to their prey and being able to get in high gear very quickly is vital. Otherwise dinner gets away.

Fortunately, cheetahs don't have to be fast all the time and actually spend most of the day sleeping and resting, like most cats. In fact, they need their amazing speed only to do two essential things—catch prey and avoid danger. It is worth pointing out that they

Speed at the right time is everything, and mistakes can be costly.

have to be fast eaters as well, otherwise larger and stronger animals are likely to not only take their food but also eat them for dessert.

The brilliantly designed cheetah is an endangered species. A big reason for this is real changes in the world around them. Farms and development are taking over much of this big cat's native habitat and reducing the availability of prey. Hunters and poachers continue to find a market for their beautiful fur. These threats are in addition to the always present danger of animal predators that might catch a cheetah off guard. As a result, the cheetah population worldwide is only about 10,000 to 15,000, of which almost all live in Africa.

Speed Matters

In the world of cheetahs, speed at the right time is everything, and mistakes can be costly. Being fast when it matters determines whether they eat and whether they and their cubs will live another day. There are plenty of other places in the natural and man-made worlds where speed at the right time is essential. Many other animals who lack brawn must survive by being either clever or fast, and humans in many of their endeavors must rely on speed to prevail.

If you are a race car fan, you know that speed matters; it is an essential ingredient in winning a race. But it matters in more than the obvious way of having a fast car, because as many races are won and lost in the pits as on the track. A fast car is certainly an essential part of the equation, but stuff happens to even the fastest and best-prepared cars during the course of a race. When it does, the pit crew has to make split-second decisions and take split-second actions to keep the car in contention.

How does a great pit crew work during a pit stop? What are their secrets for changing a car's tires, filling it with gasoline, cleaning its air vents, and making other essential adjustments in less than ten seconds?

Our organizations are also at risk of extinction or at least irrelevance if we cannot adapt to the changes around us.

Pit crews succeed by focusing on the obvious things and the little details that could go unnoticed and result in big problems. At the start and finish of the whirlwind process is, in Formula One racing terms, the "lollipop man." He or she is the person who gets the car into the pit and signals the driver when it is safe to leave. Split seconds count here.

Pit crews must also be ready for any contingency. While the race is on and the cars are zooming around the track, it might look as though they are simply hanging out waiting for the routine stops. But they are actually focused on understanding anything that could possibly go wrong and what they would do to fix it. In fact, the best pit crews spend countless hours training and practicing for any situation that could occur. The 20 or so members also focus on their specific roles and how they fit into the highly orchestrated conduct of a pit stop. Contrary to what one might imagine, the members of a top pit crew also spend countless hours getting and staying in shape so they can be quick enough and strong enough to do what needs to be done. As with cheetahs, split seconds count.

As we saw in the last chapter, speed also counts in the shock trauma center or any place else where life hangs in the balance. Speed also matters in most other business settings, too, although the implications are not typically as dramatic. Remember when Federal Express reinvented the world of package delivery? Their compelling notion that people and organizations needed things "absolutely positively overnight" launched an entire industry and changed the way customers perceive what was not only possible but also should be essential. Now we expect to be able to track our shipments at every step in the delivery process. In the same light, the Internet and advances in digital communication allow us to share critical information faster with customers, partners, and colleagues. This, in turn, has led to a dramatic decline in the traditional business of the post office as the number of people who actually write and mail letters to each other shrinks every year.

The list of settings in which speed matters and could be a compelling differentiator could go on and on. We want products more quickly, even products that are customized for us. So companies like Dell have figured out major innovations in their processes and supply chains to keep our business. We want the freshest possible food, the most up-to-date information, or the fastest turnaround for a needed repair. We want to trade a stock instantly or receive approval for a loan the moment we apply. We even want cash faster when we go to an ATM. Companies are winning by figuring out how to do all of these things. Governments are also working to figure out how to deliver services to citizens faster and more efficiently.

Speed only matters if we are brilliant at doing something the customer wants fast.

So if you think that speed doesn't matter to your business or organization, think again. Think about how you, just like the cheetah or a pit crew, will need to be designed for speed. What will you commit to doing fast? How will you be organized to get it done? Who will you have on your team? How will you be trained and prepared to deliver the compelling value you promise? Customers are demanding greater speed. Like cheetahs, our organizations are also at risk of extinction or at least irrelevance if we cannot adapt to the changes around us.

How Fast Are You When It Matters?

So what about you and your company or organization? Do you understand the role that speed plays in your ultimate success? Do you know when speed matters and what you need to do at those times to stand out from the pack?

Again, I'd like you to go back to your understanding of the customers' needs and specific requirements to think through the steps in the process of serving them and your notion of the ideal experience for them. Then look at the places where speed is an important factor. But don't think in terms of speed alone. Speed only matters if we are brilliant at doing something the customer wants fast. For example, think of the promises that many restaurants now make to provide food quickly—and I'm not talking about only fast-food restaurants. Sit-down restaurants promise lunch in 10 minutes or it is free. But what if the food that arrives in ten minutes tastes awful? Has increased speed produced greater value for us?

Commit to figuring out the essential places where speed can give your company or organization a distinct advantage and then think about how you can be brilliant in those epic interactions.

What about something like technical support? If our organization's computer system crashes, you can bet that speed matters to us. But only if it relates to getting our system up and running again. Quickly answering the phone, on its own, doesn't matter. Quickly e-mailing a preprinted address label so we can send a defective drive into the central repair facility doesn't matter. Quickly sending out a technician who is unable to solve the problem doesn't matter.

So commit to figuring out the essential places where speed can give your company or organization a distinct advantage and then think about how you can be brilliant in those epic interactions.

Take Your Own Journey

Now take your own journey. Examples of brilliant and compelling speed abound so spend a day looking for places around you where speed matters and for companies and organizations, large and small, that have figured out how to use speed to their advantage.

But first...

Start at the Zoo.

You might want to visit the cheetahs at your local zoo first. Although you aren't likely to see them going fast in this environment, you and your colleagues will at least get a sense of speed from observing their design and learning more about them. While you are there, you might look for other animals that are fast in some important way in their native environments and learn about what enables them to do things that matter quickly. This insight will help

See what they are doing to prepare for the few moments when speed really matters in their world.

you in unlocking the keys to having people and systems that get the right things done quickly. You might also enjoy watching the movie *Duma*—a fascinating (if not totally accurate) story about a boy, a cheetah, and a powerful friendship that the boy develops on his journey to return the cub to the wild.

Then Head into the Business World.

Look for places without waiting lines and places that have to meet pressing deadlines. Or look for places that run like clockwork. What makes these organizations so successful? On the other hand, what makes some of their competitors less successful?

Go to a Race.

Finally, go to a car race or watch a car race on television and pay close attention to the teams in the pits. Watch them as much as you can, even when none of the cars have come in, to see what they are doing to prepare for the few moments when speed really matters in their world.

I am in awe of cheetahs and their remarkable design, beauty, and innate genius. If only we could figure out how to use speed to get the same "killer" results for our customers when it mattered. And, if only we could figure how to do a better job of protecting these and other magnificent role models in the wild.

chapter Eleven

When Nothing Is Everything

The Big Idea:
We can win in business by being brilliant at the little things that really matter.

The Journey:
To the set of one of the most popular television shows in history—a show about absolutely nothing...

I'm never certain if art imitates life or life imitates art, but I am sure that popular culture provides compelling insight on the world of customers. I'm also sure that the everyday details of life matter to us.

For nine years, a remarkably simple and complex television show reminded us each week of the joys and frustrations of being human, although its focus was principally on the frustrations. The show *Seinfeld* was a tribute to the challenges of life in the big city through the eyes of four unique and somewhat exaggerated human characters. Thanks to reruns, nine years after the final episode aired, it remains part of our picture of the world.

When I show *Seinfeld* episodes during seminars with executives around the world, I'm amazed by how many are familiar with the sitcom and for whom it strikes a chord. Maybe as popular culture imitates life, so businesses would do well to imitate, or at least understand, the wisdom of popular culture. In this case, the nothings in our lives and the lives of those we choose to serve are everything. So let's venture onto the set of *Seinfeld* or at least into an episode, to rediscover what really matters.

New York City and around the World

The best way to get you into the mood for nothing is to start with one of the 180 episodes of *Seinfeld*. There are many great choices, but I'll pick "The Chinese Restaurant" as a good introduction. Let's get started . . .

The scene, as the name implies, is a popular Chinese restaurant on the upper west side of Manhattan. Three of the four main characters in the show—Jerry, George, and Elaine—have just arrived for a quick dinner before going to a movie. If this sounds like a situation you have found yourself in, that will make the journey a bit easier to understand. The show, with its somewhat exaggerated characters and scenes, is actually about your life and all of our lives.

The episode begins with a brief excerpt from a Jerry Seinfeld standup comedy routine. In this instance, Jerry describes an infrequent feel-

The nothings in our lives and the lives of those we choose to serve are everything.

ing of joy that someone could have when dealing with the phone company. You've made a call on a pay phone that requires more money, and as soon as you hang up the phone it starts to ring. When you pick it up, the operator tells you how much additional money to deposit. From his perspective, it is a rare moment in our relationship with a big corporation, and especially one as pervasive in our lives as the phone company, when the average citizen has the upper hand.

"Oh, I've got the money," he says with delight. Then he bangs the quarter against the phone. "It's right here."

This brief introduction suggests that a pay phone will be part of the episode that is about to unfold. In the next twenty minutes, a parade of life's nothings will occur.

Now the actual episode begins. Needless to say, the restaurant is packed and Jerry, George, and Elaine will have to wait for a table for four. But it could be worse, the maitre d' tells them it should be only about five minutes. The fourth member of the party is going to be George's date, Tatiana. George, who is generally anxious about everything in life, is anxious to call her and becomes upset when someone is using the restaurant's pay phone. So there was a connection between the opening monologue and the episode. (If you're wondering why George needed to use a pay phone, this episode is from the second season of the show around 1990, before the widespread use of cell phones.)

Time passes and Elaine, an insecure and pushy New Yorker, is getting hungrier by the minute. She is also becoming enraged as other customers who seem to have just arrived are being seated before them. We get the clear sense that the clock is ticking and the "only about five minutes" promise was given to appease them and keep them from going somewhere else. Elaine's growing frustration has gotten Jerry and George's attention, and they offer her $50 if she will eat food off of someone else's table.

George continues to fret over not being able to call Tatiana to update her on the evening's plans, but the phone is still in use. Try to recall your life in the olden days when a phone was not available at a time when you desperately needed it. Or, in contemporary terms, imagine if all circuits were busy when you needed your cell phone most urgently. In his frustration, George confesses to leaving Tatiana's apartment at a very intimate moment.

Next, Jerry sees a woman who recognizes him, but he can't remember how he knows her. They have a brief conversation in which he avoids introducing her to his friends hoping that she will introduce herself. He also talks in the generalities of someone who has no idea who they are talking with and what to converse about.

The world offers an almost limitless supply of little things in life that can go wrong.

Finally she reveals her identity. As coincidence would have it, she works with Jerry's uncle—the very same uncle Jerry lied to in order to be able to go out with his friends this evening. Guilt ensues. Imagine making up a story to get out of doing anything or to cover something up.

Now Tatiana calls the restaurant looking for George, but the maitre d' mispronounces his last name and George misses the call.

Still desperate for food, Elaine decides to pay the maitre d' $20 for a table, but it doesn't work. The three leave the restaurant just before their name is called.

In one brief episode, the writers and actors of this show have brought a relative cavalcade of nothings that matter to our attention, putting us on notice that the world offers an almost limitless supply of little things in life that can go wrong. Multiply this by 180 episodes and you get a sense of the order of magnitude of nothing that people care deeply about. They also put us on notice that these little

To many people and customers, the sum total of the little things is what absolutely matters to them. Our ability as companies and organizations to make those little things perfect is likely to determine whether we win or lose.

things can, in the minds and lives of our endearingly pathetic characters, matter in a big way.

Many other episodes are also noteworthy—as are the many Seinfeld phrases that are now part of our standard lexicon such as "Yada, yada, yada," "re-gifting," "master of your domain," "double-dipping," "no soup for you," and "not that there's anything wrong with that." The four main characters and the other regular and irregular characters make the show's theme of nothing come alive. For those who were not regular viewers, let me provide a brief sketch of Jerry, Elaine, George, and Kramer as additional background for your thinking on this journey. You've already met three of them in the Chinese Restaurant:

Jerry Seinfeld—Jerry plays himself on the show, a standup comedian who also serves as a commentator on the human condition. He tends to focus, as the show does, on the odd and common circumstances and coincidences of life, the weird behaviors of other people, and the difficulty of having a successful relationship. Jerry is also obsessed with cleanliness. While he seems to be the most normal of the group, he is extremely insecure and spends a lot of time making fun of others. He is also preoccupied with dating very attractive women but ends most relationships early on when he finds a flaw in each that is too much for him to bear. One date has a remarkable (or remarkably awkward) laugh, another eats peas one at a time, another has "man hands," while still another wears the same dress on every date.

Elaine Benes—the only woman of the four lead characters—has a few different jobs over the course of the show. These include working as a writer and editor for Pendant Publishing Company and the J. Peterman catalog and as a personal assistant to the wealthy Justin Pitt. Like Jerry, Elaine is often trying to arrange relationships with very attractive men, and although her relationships last longer they also end with some amusing problem or calamity. These relationship difficulties, coupled with the strange demands of her eccentric employers, tend to dominate her existence. Elaine is also insecure, quick-tempered, self-focused, and never very interested in other people's problems unless they affect her directly. Also, she is a bad, or "spastic," dancer.

George Costanza— as odd as the other characters are, George is the one with real problems. He has trouble finding and keeping jobs, and regularly screws up when he is given an opportunity. He also regularly screws up in relationships. George is the most insecure one among a cast of insecure people and the most neurotic in a group of neurotic people. He is always putting himself down. But he is more than simply pathetic. George is extremely stingy and has a tendency to be dishonest in many of his dealings. He often uses little lies that become much bigger lies to try to gain some advantage in his personal or work life or to get out of tough situations. This includes lying about jobs and careers to impress women or potential employers.

Then there is Kramer, Jerry's eccentric neighbor:

Cosmo Kramer—renowned for regularly making a grand entrance by sliding into Jerry's apartment. He is also known for remarkable feats of physical humor—running into things and people, flipping over things, and occasionally being stuck in the grips of inanimate objects. Unlike the others, he has no real means of support, but he has more than his share of odd schemes for making money. He also has more than his share of odd ideas for things to do (that often get others in trouble) and interior design concepts, including creating levels in his apartment. He is also a study in contrasts, shallow and disinterested in one episode and kind and thoughtful in another. He has lots of friends but few romantic relationships.

Nothing Matters

Without stretching our imaginations much, we could surmise that these characters are playing out our lives and the lives of the customers we serve. Although I'm sure that none of us would be quite as pathetic, neurotic, self-absorbed, and insecure as the cast of *Seinfeld*. Little things mean a lot. In fact, for many people and customers, the sum total of the little things is what absolutely matters to them. Our ability as companies and organizations to make those little things perfect is likely to determine whether we win or lose.

So how do we make them perfect and remarkable? Go back to the scene in the Chinese restaurant for a moment and try to think about what could have happened to make the little things go right.

Or let's take an all-too-common business example to show the challenge and potential of this idea. Let's make it an example that most of us are all too familiar with—cable TV. I'm sure that many people have had a remarkable experience receiving cable TV. I just don't know any of them. And I wasn't surrounded by many adoring fans when I recently returned my equipment to Comcast and told them they had crossed the line of my willingness to be abused by a company. So let's use this case as an illustration of what is possible, because getting cable TV service, or almost any other service, is about making a lot of nothings amount to an experience that matters. Little things that can be either positive or annoying really count.

It turns out that companies like Comcast, and I can't speak for how the company performs in all parts of the world, are remarkable at responding quickly to sales inquiries and abominable at responding to calls from people who have already signed up. In my case I got a quick response, was vigorously encouraged to buy a lot more cable TV than I need—given that I really don't need any (except that I am addicted to ESPN and any other sports channel). When we

Little things that can be either positive or annoying really count.

finally agreed that I would take the amazing promotional offer of basic cable, high-speed Internet, and local and long-distance telephone for one fabulous low monthly rate of $99 plus taxes, we then set up a time to have the installation done.

Unfortunately they were very busy. After all, an offer this good is hard to pass up, even for those of us who don't really need cable. We finally found a date that would work ten days later, and I was given a window of 8:00 AM to 12:00 noon when the installers would arrive. In a world where nothing is everything, I would have expected that they could make the installation sooner and that they might have evening or weekend times so a customer would not have to take off from work. But I'm expecting more nothing than they were prepared to offer.

> **Recognize the little things that could either make me smile or frown and commit to doing them with understanding, concern, and skill.**

I began the big day hoping that they would arrive at the start of the four-hour window, but at noon they had yet to appear. So I called the customer service number and after navigating a series of confusing prompts finally—after twenty-four minutes and fifty-seven seconds—was connected to a real person who had absolutely no idea when they would arrive other than to say that they should be at our house shortly.

Shortly turned out to be 2:15 p.m.

Upon arrival, three men surveyed our property and asked whether we'd had cable TV before. "No," I replied, "but hopefully we will have it now."

"Not exactly," one responded. "Your house is a bit too far from the road for the cable we brought. If we use this cable you're not going to get enough signal for both the TV and the Internet."

"Well, can you get the other cable now."

"Not exactly. We'll have to call our boss, have him come out to check, and then make another appointment."

By now I'm sure that you have spotted several more nothings that were starting to really matter to me but for which Comcast and its representatives were either clueless or knew about but couldn't care less.

I'd like to say the story got better, but it wasn't until the third visit two weeks later that their technicians were able to install our service. And the installation brought its own set of problems. Most significant was the fact that the installer had very little idea of how to convert our telephone service to their cable system. Maybe it was because we have an old house, or maybe it was because they lacked adequate training in a service that the company saw as essential to its growth as a part of bundled connectivity. I was always told that it is best to be reasonably competent when offering a product, service, or solution to customers. But this was obviously not part of the Comcast gameplan.

In fact, once they started messing with our phone, they rendered it inoperable and could only say, "Well, we will have to send someone back out who knows more about phones." Though one of the technicians was thoughtful enough to say that they hadn't had much (implication "any") training on installing phones in older houses. The expert arrived the following week but could not crack the code.

So we requested that they turn our service back to Verizon, a company that has made great strides to improve its customer service, and we spent the following six weeks without phone service and relied on our cell phones to keep in touch with family, friends, and the local pizza and Thai food delivery services.

We also spent the following six months being billed by Comcast for phone service that we never received. With each phone bill, I called their customer service number, waited on hold for anywhere from three to thirty-five minutes, and then explained our situation to the representative. Most representatives were cordial and said that they could understand my frustration and would have the situation resolved. But nothing would

Commit to talking with a cross-section of customers to find out what they think are the little things that mean a lot.

happen, and the bills kept coming. After a few months of not paying the phone portion of the bill, we began to receive "threatening" phone calls from Comcast. "You're delinquent in paying your full bill. Please address this immediately or we will be forced to cut off your service."

I would then call back and explain the situation and that we were not intending to pay for phone service that we didn't have. And again I was told that this would be corrected, and I assumed wrongly that it would. But one rainy night in September, a Comcast uninstaller, who was obviously unable to see our doorbell, began pounding on our door at dinnertime. "I'm here to cut off your service," he stated angrily as though we had committed a crime against the company.

"This is a surprise," I replied. "I was told by the customer service department that they were going to straighten out our account. They even apologized for treating us poorly."

"Because it's a rainy night I'll give you a break," he responded in a huff. "But I'll be back in three days to turn it off."

Once again I called Comcast and once again, after repeating the entire story, I was told that they would take care of everything. Three weeks later our service was cut off, and I gladly returned their equipment and told them that I was pleased to end one of the worst customer relationships I had ever had. A relationship in which practically every little and big thing seemed to go wrong. But maybe they never thought of it as a relationship. Maybe they thought nothing of all the "nothings" that really mattered to me.

A week later their senior customer representative called to inform me that they were correcting my bill and that she hoped we would come back to Comcast. "Not before hell freezes over," I replied.

This was such an obvious case of the little things adding up to what could have been a positive customer experience, but they added up to the worst possible experience. Most companies aren't this bad. They respond quickly to customers. They actually collect and use information provided by customers—something which Comcast admitted they did not do. There were no central records of my repeated calls and conversations. Most companies provide adequate training to deliver the products they offer so the products work. Most companies also try to correct problems quickly to keep a customer.

There are so many ways to be brilliant at the little things, especially as it relates to basic goods and services that people and companies buy, and so often that is what really matters to the customer. Recognize the little things that could either make me smile or frown and commit to doing them with understanding, concern, and skill.

Focus your creative thinking on being brilliant in these moments and situations

I should note that while Comcast was not a pure monopoly in our county, they had the principal license to provide cable service. As this is now changing, one can only imagine that the big and little things are likely to start meaning a whole heck of a lot more to them.

How Good Are You at Nothing?

So what are the nothings that matter in the life of the customers you choose to serve, and how good is your company or organization at handling them?

To figure this out, begin by looking at data on the most common issues, concerns, or complaints that you receive from customers. Don't have any organized data? Then commit to talking with a cross-section of customers to find out what they think are the little things that mean a lot. Then commit to a process of continually asking these questions and updating your knowledge. You might also want to ask them if they have ideas about how you can be brilliant in addressing them. These can be a perfect starting point for you and your team to do your own creative thinking about ways to turn an issue into a compelling positive response. Imagine that if you understood the nothings better than anyone else and were committed to thinking and acting on them then you would have a distinct advantage over your competitors.

But don't stop there. Remember when we talked about thinking through the experience of being your customer from start to finish. This type of diagnostic analysis, done with a sense of openness and curiosity, can help you to identify a more complete set of nothings that matter to those you and your company or organization choose to serve. Then you can focus your creative thinking on being brilliant in these moments and situations.

Take Your Own Journey

Now take your own journey and spend a day looking for places around you where the little things mean a lot.

Watch Your Own Episode or Two.

You can begin by watching a few episodes of *Seinfeld* as a team and taking notes on all of the nothings that drive people crazy.

Use this as the starting point for thinking about the lives of your customers and how doing business with you causes them big and little frustrations. Then zoom in on the obvious frustrations and write a new script that replaces issues with real value.

Then Head into the Business World.

Look for places that have figured out how to make challenging or complicated customer interactions go smoothly. These are likely to be businesses and activities based on large numbers of interactions or transactions just like the cable company. Find out who is good at it and pay a visit. As long as you are not a competitor, they should be open to sharing some of their secrets.

Imagine that for many customers the biggest thing we can do for them is get all of the little things right. So let's figure out how to really walk through our customer experience in their shoes.

I am a big fan of *Seinfeld* and find myself tuning in to reruns for a few minutes or a few hours at a time. Something about the misadventures and unusual genius of these odd characters gets my thinking going. It's probably because we come up with some of our best ideas when we begin by going to extremes in making the little things that matter count.

chapter TWelVe

It **Is** Rocket Science

The Big Idea:
We can win in business by being perfect, or as close to perfect as possible.

The Journey:
To the launch of an Atlas 5 rocket and the world of rocket scientists...

When faced with a challenge in our personal lives or organizations, it is common to say "it's not rocket science" or "it's not brain surgery" as though the things that most of us deal with are relatively simple and straightforward. "Just get it done" is the implication. No need to spend that much time thinking about it. We're not trying to land a person on the moon here. We're simply trying to get the service technician to show up during the nine-hour window we promised. Surely that doesn't require a PhD in aeronautical engineering?

But what if we actually behaved like rocket scientists? Would we be able to make a more compelling difference in the way we served our customers? Would the everyday challenges we face as companies and organizations be handled with greater skill and better results? I sense that the answer is *yes,* but let's take a journey to find out together by heading out to the launch pad of one of the most successful rocket programs in history to see what it takes to achieve mission success. The answer might surprise you.

January 2006: Cape Canaveral, Florida

It's "T minus two minutes and counting" to the launch of NASA's New Horizons mission. Powered by the latest generation Atlas 5 rocket, this spacecraft is about to begin a ten-year-long journey to Pluto and the Kuiper Belt, a region of ancient rock and ice bodies well beyond the orbit of Neptune. Along the way it will pass by Jupiter, making more than 700 observations of this giant planet and its four largest moons. If this sounds amazing, it is. In the heady world of rocket science, missions like these will stretch our understanding of how the universe around us is structured and how it operates in ways humans have never known before.

They will also stretch the knowledge and capabilities of a remarkable team of scientists and engineers working for NASA and many of its leading partners, including Lockheed Martin, which has led the development of the Atlas 5 rocket that will take New Horizons into space, and the Applied

To rocket scientists, there is no room for error.

Physics Lab at Johns Hopkins University, which built New Horizons—the fastest spacecraft ever launched. If everything doesn't go perfectly, this remarkable rocket, spacecraft, and journey will end abruptly on the front page of every leading newspaper in the world. To rocket scientists, there is no room for error. Years of work, development, testing, and refinement have gone into this day. In the last minutes before liftoff, the entire team will be focused and totally engaged in making its final checks and preparations.

Let's listen to some of the interchange from the control center on January 19, 2006, as provided by NASA and its partners:

"T minus two minutes and counting."

"One fifty-five." "Launch sequencer start."

"Minus one forty." "Launch enabled."

"Minus one twenty-five." "Third stage SNA armed."

"Minus one twenty." "FCF count started."

"Minus one fifteen." "Reduce ECS for launch." "Roger."

"T minus one minute and counting."

"Minus fifty-five seconds." "Third stage is go." "Roger."

"Minus forty seconds." "Stable at Step Three."

"Twenty-five seconds." "Status check." "Go Atlas." "Go Centaur."

"Fifteen seconds."

"Eleven. Ten. Nine. Eight. Seven. Six. Five. Four. Three. Two. One. We have ignition and liftoff of NASA's New Horizons spacecraft on a decade-long voyage to visit the planet Pluto and then beyond."

"T plus fifteen seconds. Everything continues to look good
    as the Atlas 5 vehicle climbs away from America's east
    coast. The five solid rocket strap-on boosters are burn-
    ing just fine carrying the New Horizons spacecraft on
    its way to the very edge of our solar system."

"T plus thirty-five seconds."

"T plus forty seconds."

"One minute into flight."

"Boosters throttled back to seventy-five percent thrust."

"T plus one minute forty-five seconds. Everything contin-
    ues to look good. Boosters have just jettisoned. Solid
    separation looks good. Main stage still running fine."

"T plus two minutes. Vehicle currently flying at thirty-
    three nautical miles altitude, thirty-nine miles down-
    range, at a speed of 4,780 miles per hour."

All in a day's work, give or take several years of planning,
development, testing, and preparation by the team of rocket

scientists who made this mission happen. But who are these people, and are they that much different than the rest of us? If so, is there anything we can learn from them that would help us to deliver greater value to the customers we choose to serve?

Mission Success and the Concept of Wing Walking

John Karas has spent his whole life thinking about rockets. His father was an original employee of Glenn L. Martin, a pioneer in aircraft design and manufacturing, and his uncles worked in the space program. So the topics of flight and rockets were always being discussed at the dinner table, and he

Rocket science is all about mission success.

had unique access to some of the leading figures in the aerospace industry. Then, as an engineering co-op student with NASA during college, he worked on the last Apollo Soyuz mission. Since that time he has worked on just about every major rocket program, including directing the Atlas 5 program. He is now Vice President for Humans in Space at Lockheed Martin, one of the world's largest defense and aerospace corporations.

The Atlas 5 program has been, arguably, the most successful rocket program in history. Not long ago I had the opportunity to talk with John and his colleague Ron Paulson, vice president for engineering at Lockheed Martin, about the real keys to success as a "rocket scientist." Their picture is a bit different than I might have imagined, given our notion of the genius of rocket scientists and fascination with the amazing contraptions they build.

To put their insight into perspective, let's start with the basic reality that rocket science is all about mission success. This means designing the rocket so it can launch a payload into space successfully, given the unique requirements and constraints of the customers and their "mission." It's not simply a matter of lighting a match and hoping it works.

Mission success is always threatened by the inevitable possibility of failure, and the essential need to avoid failure is what drives rocket scientists and the way they approach their world. This potential for failure can be catastrophic, as failure comes with a very high business cost. Not only does the rocket blow up, but you go out of business. The Titan rocket, for example, had three commercial missions. When one failed, costing $1.5 billion, it went out of production. That failure occurred not because of a serious design flaw, but because someone stepped on two wires in the final preparation prior to launch. The Atlas 1 had two failures that took General Dynamics out of the rocket business. One of those failures occurred when one small screw backed out of place. As complicated as a rocket is, it is only as good as its weakest (and sometimes smallest) part.

The most essential guiding principle for rocket scientists is "controlled evolution," a process of analysis, reanalysis, and change that results in revolutionary new developments over an extended period of time and modification.

That's why the Atlas 2, 3, and 5 family of rockets and their evolution is so impressive. As of this writing, they had achieved eighty successful missions without a single failure. In the ten-year period in which those missions took place, the rockets have gone through nine significant changes. According to John Karas, that's like building a new rocket each year for close to ten straight years. These changes have included lengthening the upper stage of the rocket, creating new and better performing "common" engines, increasing payload capacity and flexibility, upgrading the avionics, improving the types of fuel used, and increasing the number of amenities that are available to customers. None is earth-shattering, but taken together they constitute a revolution in rocket design and capability.

This means that the most essential guiding principle for rocket scientists is "controlled evolution," a process of analysis, reanalysis, and change that results in revolutionary new developments over an extended period of time and modification. The launch of New Horizons—prior to the recent controversy over whether Pluto actually is a planet—marks the latest step in that evolution. This newest version of the Atlas 5, with all of these incremental changes, is the biggest and the fastest man-made flying object ever, with an eventual speed of 56,000 miles per hour. John Karas calls this the "rule of wing walking." He elaborates, "You take small steps with not too much of a reach in between. In other words, you don't let go of one design until you have a firm grasp of the next."

Rather than being wildly innovative and coming up with totally new concepts and designs, rocket scientists are constantly pushing the edge of what they already know. Ron Paulson suggested that "amid all of the remarkable improvements we've made, rockets themselves haven't changed that much in the past fifty years—not since the days of Werner von Braun." So wing-walking genius combined with meticulous attention to detail in engineering and reengineering are the essential ingredients. That's not to say it isn't remarkable each time a rocket is launched

As complicated as a rocket is, it is only as good as its weakest (and sometimes smallest) part.

successfully. After all, we are talking about a controlled explosion in which fuel is flowing very fast, temperatures get very hot (i.e.,

2,500–4,000 degrees Celsius), and a lot of variables come into play. But the ability to eliminate the potential for error is vital.

So why keep changing in the face of this reality? Because customers and their needs continue to change and there are always "unknown unknowns," such as weather patterns, solar flares, and lightning strikes that drive rocket scientists to add greater robustness and extra factors of safety to the system. Ron Paulson emphasized that customers are always looking for more bang for their dollar through greater reliability, better performance (i.e., the ability to lift a larger payload), and reduced cost. Not to mention the amenities that John Karas spoke about, which include the ability to design or configure a spacecraft to handle a certain type of payload, different air conditioning inside (i.e., hot air, cold air, or dry air), and the ability to deliver a softer ride by tailoring the acceleration and trajectory of the rocket.

Rather than being wildly innovative and coming up with totally new concepts and designs, rocket scientists are constantly pushing the edge of what they already know.

It turns out that even rocket customers are looking for greater value all the time, and competitors in China, Russia, and Europe are also hard at work trying to figure out how to be different and better. With roughly fifty to sixty rockets being launched each year, there is no great surplus of business opportunities, though that could change. So while revolution takes time, the notion "if you're not new, you're through" is always on the minds of rocket scientists.

The Possibilities of Space

Who knows what the future will hold for rocket scientists? What we do know is that a lot more human activity is going on in space than most of us would imagine. In addition to the international space station and the periodic manned flights into space, a steady stream of rocket launches carrying commercial satellites support the world's growing appetite for telecommunications and entertainment. They also carry a wide array of imaging satellites used to track and predict weather and climate change, observe land use and land conservation, and observe or spy on other nations. Add to the list a lot of military satellites whose purposes most of us are not privy to. By one estimate, currently 800 to 1,000 satellites circle the earth, but many are now space garbage—either no longer functioning or too antiquated to meet our current needs. So in addition to new satellites for new purposes, there is a need to regularly update the satellites that are already up there.

We now think of space not only as "the final frontier" but also as a place filled with new, exciting business challenges and defense requirements. In addition to thoughts about establishing possible colonies on the moon, scientists are busy trying to determine if we can actually get people to Mars. Entrepreneurs are viewing space as a venue for a unique kind of tourist and as a possible location for the production of very specialized technical products and processes that might be possible or more cost-effective in an environment with little or no gravity. Who knows what will be going on there in fifty years? We know about the plans, at least from a political perspective if not a basic technical perspective, to use space as a place from which to defend ourselves in the event of an attack.

The ability to eliminate the potential for error is vital.

So rockets and the people who build them will continue to evolve in advance of the next revolution in space.

The Pursuit of Perfection Matters

What do rocket scientists have to teach the rest of us mortals about customer and business success? The answer probably depends on whether your company or organization is being asked to deliver products, services, and solutions that are perfect or close to perfect. Or on whether there is a real opportunity to win in your industry by delivering perfection. If either is the case, notions of controlled evolution, wing walking, and putting in place a process for eliminating the potential for failure are essential to your ability to deliver compelling value.

Notions of controlled evolution, wing walking, and putting in place a process for eliminating the potential for failure are essential to your ability to deliver compelling value.

I recently typed the words "perfect products and services" into a Google search and got more than 43 million results. Although they weren't 43 million distinctly perfect offerings, it was a response that might lead someone to believe that delivering perfection matters. The results seemed to cut across practically every industry. There were companies offering "perfect" legal software, "perfect" home theater solutions, "perfect" cups of coffee every time, "perfect" gas tanks, "perfect" Web design, "perfect" digital pictures, "perfect" single-processor servers, "perfect" engagement rings and "perfect" wedding gowns, "perfect" job interviews that would produce "perfect" job candidates, "perfect" scanners, "perfect" billing solutions, "perfect" abdominal muscle toners, "perfect" limousines, "perfect" phone services, and even "perfect" machine-made snow. If only I had a pair of perfect skis to navigate it! And this was just the tip of the perfect iceberg. It was enough perfection to make someone feel imperfect or at least inadequate.

So perfection, or at least the promise of perfection, is not a new idea. But how many of these perfect products, services, and solutions come close to delivering the compelling value they claim? Or is it simply marketing hype? And does it really matter to the customers they are trying to serve?

For some customers being perfect, or at least not failing, really does matter. These customers require a specific product, service, or solution to maintain their lives or their organization's viability. This includes such things as:

- Vaccines or other essential medicine that enable people to survive or manage their condition;
- Sources of power (or at least back-up generators) that keep life-sustaining equipment running;
- Computer systems that can't afford to go down or be hacked because they contain vital data;
- Social security checks that are essential for retirees to buy food or pay the rent;
- Alarm systems that protect people and other things of value;
- Communication networks for troops in battle or during an emergency; and
- Motor vehicles that need to keep us safe.

And, I'm sure, many other things. But the common denominators seem to be health, safety, life, and a set of business necessities.

So think about whether your company or organization fits in this category. If it does, think about how you do things when you can't afford to fail.

First, you do a lot of analysis and planning to account for everything that could possibly go wrong. Then you develop a detailed prototype that you can thoroughly test. And you use the best available knowledge and technology to guide you. But technology is only a set of rules about what we know, not what we don't know. So all of your people need to make good decisions along the way that take into account the limitations of their knowledge and their best understanding of the risks those limitations bring and how to minimize those risks.

Successful rocket science requires the right combination of technical expertise, the right technology, the right people, the right tools, processes, and systems, the right culture and attitude, the right sense of curiosity, and the right leadership to pull it all together. In a sense, this is the very same formula that makes most enterprises successful, but the demand that there is no room for error sets these guys and gals apart. It also requires curiosity and always asking, "Will this really work? Can we make it better?"

These are reasonable questions for all of us to ask. In fact, the ability to achieve something close to perfection from the customer's standpoint, while not always essential, can be a powerful strategy for being different and delivering more compelling value than competitors.

The implication from rocket scientists is that we can only be perfect if we are focused on making incremental change. This is fine for companies and organizations offering products that are acknowledged industry leaders in fields where only modest change is expected or desired in the short term. If we want to try something new and radically different, however, we have to be willing to accept mistakes and imperfection.

But hold on, we can still apply the notion of controlled evolution in a meaningful way once we launch a new product or service by making sure the initial offering is credible and then quickly hanging out with the customers to find out what improvements and amenities they really need. Then we can beat the clock to try to "evolve" them and lock in that quality.

Think about big-screen televisions and the competing technologies in the market. There are front and rear projection sets, plasma televisions, liquid crystal or LCD displays, and even digital light processor, or DLP, displays. When each was introduced, it was heralded as a real breakthrough—but a breakthrough with flaws. Yet these works in progress from world-class companies, such as Sony, Panasonic, Samsung, and others, found customers looking for the next great thing and willing to tolerate a less than perfect product. Not that these products failed regularly, but they certainly had room for improvement in terms of picture quality, color quality, and the overall entertainment experience. As a result, their manufacturers quickly switched into a faster mode of wing walking.

Take computer software for example. How many major software products get it right the first time? Not many (or any). How many new versions of complex software are perfect? Old bugs are fixed, but new bugs tied to new user requirements appear and necessitate regular updates, or wing walking, to address legitimate customer concerns. Windows was never perfect and yet it led the market. Will the conversion to Vista hold the promise of something closer to perfection in a world of moving targets? And what is perfection in the software? I can imagine a software product that runs itself, never has problems, and actually makes my computer healthier. But I'm not sure that controlled evolution will ever get us there.

Commit to figuring out how to make incremental changes that matter with an eye toward transforming your offerings and achieving a much higher level of customer satisfaction.

Is Perfection within Your Reach?

So what about you and your company or organization? Does perfection or the pursuit of perfection really matter to those you choose to serve? And, if so, how would you define it in your marketplace?

If it's not rocket science, you should be able to be the best at what you do. The real challenge is to figure out how to put the right discipline in place to quickly evolve your product, service, or solution. Commit to figuring out how to make incremental changes that matter with an eye toward transforming your offerings and achieving a much higher level of customer satisfaction. Or commit to rethinking your offerings and changing the game with a new product, service, or solution that is credible enough to deliver real value, backed by a promise to work with your customers to get it right as quickly as possible. Then put in process a way to assure flawless delivery.

Take Your Own Journey

Now take your own journey. As I noted above, promises of perfection abound. Your job is to find examples that really mean something and adapt their knowledge to your company or organization.

Here are some ideas for getting you going . . .

Take a Test Drive.

Head out into the world around you with your eyes wide open to claims of products, services, or solutions that are "perfect" or striving to be perfect. You might start at the local Lexus dealer because they advertise a commitment to "the relentless pursuit of perfection." After all, if their cars are so great, they might even convince you to buy one. But at least find out how they continually innovate to create a better car and driving experience. You might even ask to test drive the car that claims to be able to parallel park itself. Try to figure out their secret recipe for delivering perfection.

Then Look for Three More Role Models.

You might start by thinking about places where perfection really matters. Then look for companies or organizations with products, services, or solutions comparable to yours (but in different industries) that are focused on the highest quality and the fewest defects. The ones who pledge to "get it right the first time." Now figure out what they do to achieve their promise and what wings they had to walk on to achieve greater customer success.

Will this really work?
Can we make it better?

We tend to think of the people who build rockets in reverent terms. After all, they are so much more sophisticated than the rest of us. But I left Lockheed Martin with a clear sense that when applying our genius to anything that really matters we should all say, "It *is* rocket science!"

chapter Thirteen

No Smile, No Gain

The Big Idea:

We can succeed in business by making customers happier and healthier.

The Journey:

To an exercise class on the North Sea where the focus is on having fun inside and out ...

Fitness matters, whether we like to admit or not. When we are in good shape, we have the best chance to be effective. Our bodies and our minds are able to do more things well. Still many, if not most, of us have a love-hate relationship with exercise. We struggle to make it happen on a regular basis even though we know that it is good for us, and we often look for excuses to take a day off from jogging, lifting weights, going to an aerobics class, swimming our favorite stroke, trying to keep our balance on the treadmill, or simply taking a brisk walk. Then, hopefully, we get over the hurdle and reach a point where the initial torture is now easier, more rewarding and almost essential to our peace of mind. We might even begin to think that exercise is fun.

In an important sense, customers would like to be fitter, too. They would love it if getting in better shape was also fun. But the two rarely seem to go hand in hand. They, too, long to be more energetic, more focused, and more capable of getting the right things done, but it is equally hard for them to get over the hump. Is it possible that we could learn something about customer success from an organization that has created its own unique and compelling approach to personal well-being? The organization is Friskis&Svettis, and in a country where health and fitness seem to matter, they have developed a cult-like following. So let's put on our workout clothes and head out for our morning exercise and a smile.

Bovallstrand, Sweden

It's 9:00 AM on a beautiful summer morning in the delightful village of Bovallstrand on the west coast of Sweden. When I say beautiful, I'm not exaggerating. Clear blue skies, a light breeze coming off the water, and over nineteen hours of daylight in the middle of the summer. The air temperature is about 68 degrees Fahrenheit (or 20 degrees Celsius), and the water temperature is slightly warmer, about 71 degrees Fahrenheit (or 21.5 degrees Celsius) on this late July day.

Now imagine getting ready to exercise in a beautiful park surrounded by dramatic rock formations and overlooking a majestic part of the North Sea called the Skagerrak. The Skagerrak is actually a strait running between Norway, the southwest coast of Sweden, and the Jutland Peninsula of Denmark. It is a place filled with a rich history. From this vantage point, a quick scan of the landscape reveals fifteen to twenty beautiful rocky islands, some only a few hundred meters from the shores, boats of all shapes and sizes, and some birds that look almost prehistoric.

This is the predicament that we find ourselves in as the Friskis&Svettis class is about to begin. We could have come to this spot to simply take in the view, but instead we and thirty-five other people are here to work our tails off, and we plan to enjoy it. Otherwise the people behind this "keep fit" association will not be very happy. The participants this morning are a quietly enthusiastic group of people from Bovallstrand and the surrounding villages. Some are locals who live here year-round; they are people who either grew up in this part of Sweden or have chosen to leave the big cities of Gothenburg and Stockholm for a more relaxed pace. Others are summer guests, trying to relax, reconnect, and get back into the physical and psychological shape required to begin another year of work. Most are women, ranging in age from teens to sixties. Beyond that, they are not a diverse group, but remember, this is rural Sweden.

The instructor, a forty-two-year-old woman named Lotta, turns on the music and offers a quick welcome. "I'm very happy to have you join me this morning," she says in Swedish. "It is a perfect day to exercise and to have a smile," she continues. "Find your own pace as you follow along."

It is also not a stretch to imagine that the "healthiest" customers can make the greatest use of, or derive the greatest value from, our products, services, and solutions with the least amount of customer care.

Then the class begins. Lotta appears to be the human embodiment of fitness—relatively tall, thin, strong, focused, coordinated, apparently without an ounce of body fat, and really into the whole experience. She is wearing an official red Friskis&Svettis T-shirt, matching shorts, and what must be a special pair of aerobic shoes. I say that because my athletic shoes are not nearly as capable of doing the exercises she does so effortlessly. But seriously, the shoes don't make the man or woman.

Lotta seems born to exercise. Just as some of us are meant to read a book, play a musical instrument, or watch sports and drink premium-quality malt beverages. Hers is a body to die for. Although in my case, I am striving (somewhat less successfully) for the male equivalent.

After a brief warm-up, we get going into more strenuous exercise, with Swedish and American music pounding in the background. The beat is constant and helpful, but after fifteen to twenty minutes I am already working very hard. In fact, the entire class, which lasts about an hour, is quite a workout. In the process we will work on fitness and tone, then focus and balance, then strength and stamina, then coordination, and then cool-down and relaxation to get centered. Each component provides its unique challenges. Quite remarkably everyone, no matter what their ability, seems to be having fun. And that is what makes this hour so weird and compelling.

The real challenge of Friskis&Svettis, it seems, is not to create the perfect body or to become the world's best-conditioned athlete, though many of the participants are in very good shape. Instead, it is to experience the joy of becoming healthier by appreciating the importance of fitness on our own terms. The fun and smile result when we find ourselves getting hooked and feeling the real benefit.

I should note that when the class ends some of the participants head off for a five-kilometer run (roughly three miles for those of you who think in nonmetric terms). The rest of us will jump into the North Sea for a refreshing swim.

Friskis&Svettis, a rare nonprofit association with over 15,000 leaders, instructors, and hosts in a country where the government takes care of most things, is now a Swedish institution. Founded in Stockholm in 1978, its first class attracted only one participant. Today, however, the association has more than 417,000 members, with affiliates all across Sweden, and in Norway, Finland, Denmark, Belgium, France, the Netherlands, Luxembourg, and Scotland.

The organization's mission is simple—to provide pleasurable and easily accessible high-quality exercise for everyone. Its objective is to encourage as many people as possible to adopt a positive and active lifestyle by seeing exercise as something that is fun. If people enjoy exercising, they are likely to want to do it over and over again—and they are likely to smile when they think about the possibility of exercise.

Is there more that our product, service, or solution could actually deliver if the customer was more knowledgeable?

At the core of Friskis&Svettis's program is a workout called *jympa,* a concept based on music, the joy of motion, and positive leadership. This is the basic class that my cohorts and I take overlooking the sea. The organization has even adapted the jympa concept to meet the needs of people with disabilities or injuries and women who are pregnant. Older people simply adapt their level to the programs available. Age doesn't seem to be much of an issue. We recently attended a class in another coastal town called Smögen. The class was led by a Danish instructor who must have been 70 years old. He was, without question, the fittest seventy-year-old I have ever tried in vain to keep up with.

The fact that Friskis&Svettis is a Swedish invention is not particularly surprising given the nature of Swedish government and society. After all, this is a country that brought us Volvos, Saabs, the Nobel prize, a wholesome image of healthy blonde people, and marinated fish. It is also a country that is generally at the top of rankings for the longest life expectancy, best quality of life, and greatest environmental awareness. Sweden is a rare mix of capitalism and socialism, where taxes are extremely high and the government provides a wide range of social services, including education, unemployment protection, and healthcare. But socialized medicine comes with caveats and limitations. To work effectively it must be part of a culture in which staying healthy takes precedence over getting sick and visiting the doctor. The more each citizen gets sick, the greater the cost to society. The system is not equipped to provide a lot of care to everyone. So citizens must take more responsibility for their own health rather than relying on healthcare providers. In this environment, exercise really matters—not that exercise shouldn't always matter in any environment. There is also a strong sense of culture here, of being Swedes, and of conforming in good and less good ways. Once someone you know buys into an idea, others are likely to be inclined to accept it as well.

Obviously, Sweden is not the only place where fitness is an obsession. Aerobics and other forms of exercise have become big business around the globe, with gyms and classes springing up everywhere. Yet by some measures America and many parts of the world

We could eventually measure our success by our ability to make the customer smile when they were using our product.

have more unfit people than ever before. And it seems we're doing a good job of "supersizing" the rest of the planet.

Fitness and Well-Being Matter

Just as it is not a stretch to assume that the healthiest people require the least amount of healthcare, it is also not a stretch to imagine that the "healthiest" customers can make the greatest use of, or derive the greatest value from, our products, services, and solutions with the least amount of customer care. By making an upfront investment in their "health"—i.e., their knowledge about how to use our offerings and then committing to being available when and if they really need us—we can be compelling in a different way. Like the people at Friskis&Svettis, we can try to make it something that is enjoyable as well.

How do we make customers healthier, happier, and more successful? We can begin by thinking about what "health" or "fitness" might mean in the relationship between our customers and the products, services, and solutions we provide them. In simple terms, it means that the things we offer should do what they are intended to do. But that is only a starting point for enabling customers to derive extra value and well-being from their use. Is there more that our product, service, or solution could actually deliver if the customer was more knowledgeable? Greater functionality. Better results. More peace of mind. How many customers are content to barely scratch the surface of what is possible?

Unlock real value by making the customer healthier and reducing the likelihood that they will need costly and disruptive healthcare for the things that don't have to ail them.

Software is a classic example. Customers typically buy it to do a particular job or perform a specific function, and few come close to tapping its full potential. What if software companies committed to teaching their customers how to unlock more value by making them smarter about all of the product's capabilities through classes, coaching, a clearer and more engaging manual, or an upbeat tutorial with online updates offering new insight from their staff and other users? And that is just the tip of the iceberg. What if they customized the learning experience to the range of worlds and industries that customers live and operate in? After all, the better we know them and their specific condition, the "healthier" we can probably make them. If we became really good at this, we could eventually measure our success by our ability to make the customer smile when they were using our product. Their growing confidence and competence would be a personal cause for celebration.

Remember Whole Foods Market? Like Friskis&Svettis, they are on a mission to help people lead healthier lives in a very direct way. They understand that people who eat healthy food are likely to feel better, and when they feel better they are likely to buy more healthy food. This is actually the opposite, if there is such a thing, of a vicious cycle. But to help people get over the hurdle of product cost, they need to pump up their value equation and that involves making customers smarter and more comfortable about the connection between their offerings and personal success. This means having a store that is filled with important information about healthy eating and health, having a staff that is expert in the products they offer, offering classes on healthful cooking, providing a wide array of written materials on healthy and natural foods and products and how they can be cooked or used to promote a healthy lifestyle, being engaged in promoting healthy lifestyles in the communities in which they operate, and making their stores a gallery of beautiful and delectable healthy food and cuisine.

If we broaden our understanding of the notion of "health," we can adapt this model to practically any business or organization, including car companies, energy companies, financial institutions, or even plumbers and other service/repair firms. Car companies can do a better job of educating their customers on how to drive and maintain their cars more effectively in order to improve performance, increase fuel efficiency, and minimize harmful emissions. They can help teach people how to be better drivers or how to get the most out of the car's entertainment system. If they want to stretch their thinking even more, they can provide guidance, based on greater knowledge of the lifestyles and interests of market segments, on how to get more out of life with your specific vehicle as part of the equation. After all, the type of vehicle we drive says a lot about the type of lifestyle we either have or aspire to.

Energy companies can go beyond the rhetoric of promoting energy efficiency and take a far more proactive stance. They are currently the keepers of a dwindling resource, and rather than milking it and us for every last penny, they should be focused on maximizing our efficient use of existing energy sources and engaging us in a substantive journey to discover future sources. Instead, most of them bring us clever slogans and a modest investment in a sustainable future. If they really cared, they would be teaching us more about public transportation, efficient land-use planning, smaller vehicles, lowering our thermostats, and walking and riding bicycles whenever possible. In the process, they would be making all of us quite a bit healthier in the personal and global sense. However, just as most companies have a narrow view of health, energy companies have a narrow view of energy. I don't know about you, but I am assuming that most of us would like to have greater comfort that our children and grandchildren won't be forced to battle over the last drops of oil.

As far as I know, very few companies have ever lost business by making their customers smarter and fitter.

Service providers can win in the marketplace by teaching us how to keep our heating, air conditioning, plumbing, and other systems running smoothly and efficiently. They can create a financial incentive for us and themselves. But only the best think this way. Imagine a plumber committed to making you and your plumbing system much healthier. Highly unlikely, you say. Plumbers typically come when we have a crisis. At their best, they serve us by solving the problem, cleaning up their mess, and then, hopefully, not charging us an unfair price. Then they wait for us to call them again. At their worst, they do a less than adequate job, leave a mess, and charge us an outrageous amount. They capitalize on the fact that finding a good plumber is a challenge.

What if they decided to be consultants in the thoughtful use and maintenance of our plumbing systems? What if they decided to charge us an annual fee to assure that our systems were functioning properly? Now the equation would be different. Now they would be determined to get our systems running smoothly and to educate us on the most proper maintenance to avoid a catastrophe. They would probably give us a checklist and calendar with things to do on a regular basis to protect the system. They might even counsel junior on fun alternatives to throwing massive amounts of junk down the toilet. That way their job would be more routine and we would be more inclined to smile when thinking about plumbing. I bet that plenty of people would rather pay to be "fit" and go with the flow (so to speak) than need the plumbing equivalent of quadruple bypass surgery.

Start by figuring out your best opportunities to help them to get more out of the products, services, and solutions you offer them.

You can apply this example to a wide range of businesses and membership organizations. Each has the potential to unlock real value by making the customer healthier and reducing the likelihood that they will need costly and disruptive healthcare for the things that don't have to ail them. In the process they have the ability to bring a smile to the faces of healthier and more satisfied customers. By taking plumbing or any service problem off the table, we change the equation for those we choose to serve who, in turn, have a real choice about who they choose to serve them.

Smiles matter. In fact, sometimes we can win by creating a smile in the midst of an imperfect experience. Let's take airline travel. For most people, it is a necessary evil. They need to fly to get somewhere to do business or to enjoy a vacation. Few of us buy a ticket for the flying experience alone. But at least two of the most successful airlines in the world—Southwest and Virgin Atlantic—have decided that there is a chance to add value by injecting fun into the equation. As a low-cost carrier, Southwest taps into the "cattle car" mentality by training its people to be upbeat, engaging, and humorous, offering fun twists on typical in-flight communications and passenger instructions and a hearty can-do attitude within their parameter of cost. As a premium airline, Virgin Atlantic has focused on lifestyle and a more sophisticated brand of humor and service that is intended to change the equation for its customers. They challenge customers to think of the travel experience more broadly, from going to the airport by limousine or motorcycle to leaving after a massage and shower—ready to face the world healthier and better prepared.

Customers long to get things done, and our ability to make them more fit to succeed can be a differentiator worth smiling about.

Think about Friskis&Svettis. Their offerings are simple—classes and coaching to help people stay fit and enjoy the process. It is all about becoming smarter and more capable as customers. That is a compelling idea for all of us. As far as I know, very few companies have ever lost business by making their customers smarter and fitter. But few think of the world this way.

Do You Make Your Customers Smarter and Healthier?

So think about how you could make your customers smarter, healthier, and happier and how their increased knowledge and "health"—broadly defined—could benefit both of you.

Start by figuring out your best opportunities to help them to get more out of the products, services, and solutions you offer them. Could you train or mentor them to gain a quick and valuable level of fluency? Could you provide coaching so they know how to do cool things by tapping the full functionality of your offerings? Could you help them create a customized game plan for their improved "fitness" as a result of effectively using your product, service, or solution, followed by regular "check-ups" along the way to see how well they are progressing? Have fun making the connection between your business and the straightforward work of Friskis&Svettis. Think of all the relevant corollaries that might exist between an exercise-based organization and its routine and your potential routine in working to deliver value to your customers.

Again, start by being crystal clear about what your customers hope to accomplish, first with your offerings and then in a broader sense of achieving their overall mission. This picture can give you the best sense of how to build your role in making them as healthy and smart as possible.

In terms of putting a smile on your customers' faces, think about the power of Friskis&Svettis's fundamental proposition that our growing skill and confidence with exercise can bring a sense of happiness. Then, with this as your frame of reference, try to figure out fun and creative ways to build your customers' confidence in their own effectiveness. It could be a good time to test your sense of humor.

Take Your Own Journey

Now take your own journey. Start at your own fitness club or any organization that exists to make its customers or members healthier, smarter, or both and figure out what they do well and how they do it consistently.

Then Head into the Business World.

Look for places like Whole Foods that are focused on their customers' well-being and commit to hanging out there and learning as much as you can about the details of what they do. Then stretch your thinking to find three other businesses that are focused on health in a way that makes its customers smile and figure out what you can learn from them. Cast a wide net in an effort to unlock the real formula. Many of these are likely to be businesses or organizations where people go to feel better about themselves and where they get a lot of support and encouragement. They could be the most effective weight-loss centers or schools that teach people new skills. They could also be associations where people go to enjoy and develop their hobbies or interests.

Customers long to get things done, and our ability to make them more fit to succeed can be a differentiator worth smiling about.

I look forward to Friskis&Svettis each summer and increasingly to all exercise (other than the treadmill) as an opportunity to be healthier on a number of levels. I always smile when the class is done—probably because it is over, but possibly because in their everyday genius they have helped me to tap an important part of the potential for better health and joy that lives in all of us.

chapter Fourteen

Spider Sense

The Big Idea:

We can succeed in business by anticipating customer needs and responding with compelling value.

The Journey:

To the pages of a remarkable comic book and the world of a very human superhero . . .

We all know that our customers face challenges and potential opportunities every day and that their success and ours depends in large measure on our ability to help them to address each with skill and often speed. What makes this a difficult proposition is the reality that things often come up at the last minute, driving all of us into the reactive mode. It's a mode in which it is hard for most humans and organizations to do their best.

But what if we could anticipate the challenges and opportunities that our customers face? What if we could stop danger as it was unfolding rather than once it happened? What if we could see real opportunities before others do? Let's imagine that we could, because it is not just the stuff of science fiction. To really understand what we would have to do, let's take a journey to a world where we can sense when bad things are about to happen and an uncomfortable hero with the ability to stop the bad guys right in their tracks.

1962: Wherever Bad Guys Can Be Found

Spider-Man, the creation of writer Stan Lee and artist Steve Ditko, was an idea that almost didn't happen. Lee presented the concept to his publisher at Marvel Comics, but the publisher did not think that readers would like or be able to relate to a superhero that was a spider. As a concession, he agreed to publish the first Spider-Man story in a comic called *Amazing Fantasy* that was about to be discontinued, and, as they say, the rest is history. Over the past forty-five years, Spider-Man has become one of the most famous and popular superheros ever. So let's start at the beginning . . .

In the initial Spider-Man story, we meet Peter Parker, a nerdy high school student who wears glasses, enjoys studying, and is very unpopular. While attending a school field trip (something even future superheros do) to a science exhibition on radiation, Peter is bitten on the hand by an irradiated spider that subsequently dies. Peter begins to feel sick and soon starts to develop spider-like abilities. These include super strength and agility. He also develops the ability to cling to most surfaces and, most important for our purposes here, "spider sense"—the ability to sense impending danger.

The more we know about customers, prospects, and their world, the more we are likely to be able to anticipate the emerging challenges and opportunities they will face.

While initially he is unclear about how to use his super powers, Peter does makes himself a cool uniform—an essential requirement to be an actual superhero— and uses his talent for science to build a pair of wrist-mounted mechanical devices that are capable of shooting sticky web-making material.

But Peter isn't really interested in stopping criminals. Instead, lured by the prospect of money and fame, he decides to become a professional wrestler on television—another field in which cool uniforms matter—and wins his first match against a wrestler named Crusher Hogan. But fiction, and sometimes real life, has a way of helping us change our priorities. After the wrestling match, Peter let's a robber who has just stolen some money escape from the television station. He uses the excuse that it is simply not his problem. Unfortunately, the very same robber goes on to kill his guardian, Uncle Ben. When Peter realizes that he could have actually prevented Uncle Ben's death by stopping the robber back at the station, he commits himself to fighting injustice. He is driven by his own guilt and his uncle's now famous guidance:

"With great power there must also come great responsibility."

Spider-Man the superhero is born.

In the ensuing adventures, Peter uses his remarkable powers to battle a seemingly never-ending series of bad guys that includes the Burglar, the Chameleon, the Vulture, Doctor Octopus, Terrible Tinkerer, Sandman, the Lizard, Electro, the Enforcers, and Doctor Doom. The end of 1963 brought the introduction of three of Spider-Man's greatest foes—Mysterio, Green Goblin, and Kraven the Hunter. And more villains would follow.

Through it all, Spider-Man develops as the most unlikely superhero. Initially he is a teenager with all the issues that teenagers face. In fact, what makes Spider-Man so appealing is that he is among the most human of the superheros. He is an unimposing figure who wears glasses and is not really a tough guy. He shows a wide range of emotions, is vulnerable, makes mistakes, doesn't always have perfect relationships with women or others, is not always trusted by society to be a good guy, and is not always comfortable with his lot in life. He is also alone much more of the time than many other superheros. While many of the leading superheros have sidekicks with whom they can talk or use as an alter ego (e.g., Batman and Robin), Spider-Man does not. He often spends time talking to himself in rather drawn-out monologues.

He does, of course, have some pretty awesome powers, but for the most part they aren't any more spectacular than those of other renowned superheros. The graphic below gives a brief summary of some well-known superheros and their superpowers.

Some superheros and Their Superpowers

Superhero	Creator	Superpowers
Spider-Man	Stan Lee, Steve Dasko	Spider sense; ability to stick to things; great strength; night vision; speed and agility; ability to make spider webs with web-shooters.
Superman	Jerry Siegel, Joe Shuster	"Faster than a speeding bullet"; ability to fly; "more powerful than a locomotive"; can "leap tall buildings in a single bound"; X-ray vision; super-breath; invulnerability.
Batman	Bob Kane, Bill Finger	Great intelligence and conditioning; master of martial arts; superior strength; a brilliant detective; acrobatics; ability to escape. Also has cool equipment/technology.
Captain America	Joe Simon, Jack Kirby	Perfectly conditioned; great strength; speed; agility and durability; master of martial arts and other fighting styles; great intelligence; tactical and command skill; indestructible shield.
Captain Marvel	C.C. Beck, Bill Parker	"SHAZAM"—the wisdom of Solomon, strength of Hercules, stamina of Atlas, power of Zeus, courage of Achilles, and speed of

		Mercury. Also the ability to fly and cast magical spells.
The Hulk	Stan Lee, Jack Kirby	Incredible strength, stamina, and invulnerability; great leaping ability; resistance to injury; ability to regenerate damaged body parts; superior hearing.
Wonder Woman	William Moulton Marston, Sadie Holloway Marston	Ability to fly at supersonic speeds; amazing strength and stamina; great intelligence, including the ability to speak many languages; superior hearing and vision; great healing abilities. Also has cool weapons such as the "lasso of truth."
Plastic Man	Jack Cole	Ability to stretch body to amazing shapes and sizes; amazing flexibility and coordination; ability to disguise himself; can redistribute body parts and functions to become invulnerable. Possibly immortal.
Aquaman	Paul Norris, Mort Weisinger	Ability to breathe air or water; super strength and durability; ability to see in almost total darkness; mental telepathy; amazing hearing; ability to cause tidal waves.

*Source: Marvel Comics, D.C. Comics.

As I'm sure you have gathered, superheros are characters who can do things that mere mortals can't do. Think of Superman, one of the most famous superheros and one of the first modern superheros. He was the everyday guy who was "faster than a speeding bullet, more powerful than a locomotive, able to leap tall buildings in a single bound," and who, "disguised as Clark Kent (fought) a never-ending battle for truth, justice, and the American way." We mere mortals pale by comparison.

Or do we?

I should note that we tend to think of superheros as a relatively modern invention, beginning with the creation of Superman in 1938, but they have probably been around throughout much of recent human history. The Greeks created their own superheros—gods and goddesses—by magnifying the good and desirable qualities of mere mortals. Take Zeus, the king of the gods. He possessed great power that included thunder and the lightning bolt. These were certainly a reasonable equivalent to being as powerful as a locomotive in his time and not a bad differentiator from your basic human. Athena possessed remarkable wisdom, technical insight, and cunning as a strategic thinker. She could have probably figured out how to make some classical web-shooters if given the chance and might even have been a respected management consultant.

The Romans also had gods, and the Norse people had literally dozens of gods to help them explain an array of natural phenomena and human conditions that did

Think creatively about problems that could be prevented or quickly resolved and the opportunities that could be exploited.

not lend themselves directly to conversation over a beer. We can find in the folklore of many other civilizations tales of people with superhuman powers that could be used for good or evil. Like their modern counterparts, they also had very cool uniforms, but they did not change into them in a phone booth.

Superpowers Matter

So what if we could have superpowers as companies and organizations? What would we want them to be and how could we use them to create compelling value for the customers we choose to serve?

Here are some desired superpowers that regularly come up in my work with a wide range of companies:

- The ability to anticipate danger (or problems);
- The ability to eliminate danger before it happens;
- The ability to anticipate and seize opportunities;
- The ability to turn back time;
- The ability to be everywhere at any time (i.e., to be "ubiquitous"—a word that I promised my eleventh-grade English teacher I would use someday as an adult);
- The ability to be faster than a speeding bullet or at least as fast as a cheetah;
- The ability to make amazing things happen instantly;
- The ability to speak and communicate with everyone on the planet;
- The ability to speak and communicate with every creature on the planet;
- The ability to fit into and through small places without being noticed;
- The ability to always hear our customers' concerns;
- The ability to always hire incredibly talented and committed people;
- The ability to come up with the best new ideas well ahead of competitors; and

• The ability to make every customer smile.

Now let's imagine that all these powers are within our grasp if we have a commitment to make them happen. And let's use "spider sense" as our example. It turns out that the more we know about customers, prospects, and their world, the more we are likely to be able to anticipate the emerging challenges and opportunities they will face. It would be awesome if we could do this innately, but unlike superheros, mere mortals have to work hard to do super things. So let's figure it out.

We start by committing to hanging out with the customers and getting to know them as well as possible. This means living in their world and experiencing what they experience. It also means understanding their plans, objectives, and constraints and the role that our products, services, or solutions can and do play in enabling them to get important stuff done. It also means paying attention to how they use our offerings in trying to generate value. We add to this a commitment to pay closer attention to the world around them and everything that is going on, or might be going on, that affects their business. Knowing these things gives us a lot of information that we can use to think creatively about problems that could be prevented or quickly resolved and the opportunities that could be exploited.

Pick a framework for delivering compelling value and then create a superhero who can make it happen with the requisite set of talents or superpowers.

There is a compelling logic to having this as the last journey, because in addition to its big idea we can also apply the notion of superheros and superpowers to each of the other nine journeys and to practically any problem or opportunity our companies or organizations face. Pick a framework for delivering compelling value and then create a superhero who can make it happen with the requisite set of talents or superpowers. Then commit to turning your people into that very superhero or a team or army of them. It is not as hard as you might think.

If you are stuck, try thinking about how to be the worst at anticipating danger and opportunity and then turn that formula on its head.

Similarly, you can pick a problem that your organization faces and create a superhero with the powers needed to solve it. Then figure out what humans would have to do to model those powers. That is why Spider-Man is such a great example. He's really a lot like the rest of us. So there is hope for humans and the organizations we work in! If anything, however, most of us feel that we lack the power to make a change let alone do remarkable things for our customers. And this is what the discussion in Part III is intended to address.

How about a few "real world" examples? One is Staples, the office superstore that uses information technology to anticipate customer needs. Diligently analyzing customer buying patterns, they try to determine their likely future product requirements. Staples can use intimate knowledge of the past and present to predict the future and minimize the likelihood that they will be short of a product that matters to their customers. Although they are among the most sophisticated, they are not alone, as most companies forced to purchase inventory have to make decisions on a regular basis. The challenge is to figure out what information matters most.

Take our rocket scientists. They and others like them who live in a world where failure is not an option must create a multitude of scenarios and possibilities in order to prevent potential problems or to determine timely and effective responses. How often do you and your organization commit to creating scenarios for the future that you use to inform your actions?

Can You Anticipate the Future?

Hopefully, you are getting the sense that the main difference between you and most superheros is the lack of cool costumes. And you might also want to do something fun with what you wear. But for now let's focus on your ability to anticipate the future and what you are currently doing to give yourselves a chance to have spider sense.

How well do you know your customers and their world? How well do you know what is going on in the broader world that could affect their business, livelihood, or objectives in buying a product, service, or solution like yours? What steps can you take to get up to speed quickly and effectively? If you are stuck, try thinking about how to be the worst at anticipating danger and opportunity and then turn that formula on its head. For each way that you and your colleagues can figure out how to screw up, determine the opposite and use that as a great starting point for putting your predictive capabilities in place. Then think about what it would take to create an organization that works together to anticipate customer needs before they arise.

Think about what it would take to create an organization that works together to anticipate customer needs before they arise.

But don't stop there. Commit to figuring out what other "superpowers" make a compelling difference to the customers you serve. Then figure out how to master them through careful planning, thoughtful action and collaboration, and possibly a well-designed, hand-mounted, value-creating device.

Take Your Own Journey

Now take your own two-part journey . . .

Watch Your Own Movie.

Go to the video store and rent one of the classic superhero movies. Then create an afternoon event for the team that includes watching the film, accompanied with appropriate refreshments, and afterward having an upbeat discussion and working session.

Watch the film to focus on the specific superpowers of the heroes. This might even extend to the superpowers of the villains. Then look for the connection between these powers and the character's objectives and motivation. Commit to figuring out what superpowers would give your company or organization a distinct competitive edge and figure out the details of how to make it happen!

Then Head into the Business World.

Look for places in which companies or organizations are making amazing claims that are almost too "super" to be true. Then try to figure out if they are real and what it takes to make good on them. You might want to revisit our thinking about the (super)power of an unconditional guarantee.

As amazing as superheros are, they are really not much different than you and all of the other geniuses you work with, give or take some well-tailored spandex. So sharpen your superpowers and set yourself apart from the pack.

I am a big fan of Spider-Man because he demonstrates the potential for mere mortals to rise to the occasion. He is a lot more like you and your colleagues than you might have ever imagined. That creates a pretty compelling opportunity for genius to occur.

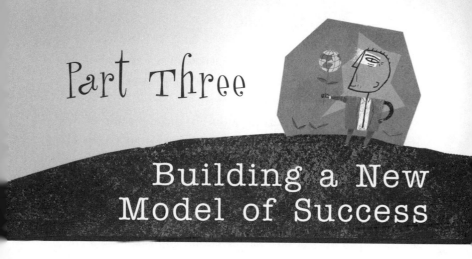

Part Three

Building a New Model of Success

Where there is an open mind, there will always be a frontier.
—Charles F. Kettering

"There is no use trying," said Alice.
"One can't believe impossible things."
"I dare say you haven't had much practice," said the Queen.
"When I was your age, I always did it for half an hour a day.
Why, sometimes I've believed as many as six impossible things
before breakfast."
—Lewis Carroll

Now it is time to make sense of our journeys. Like many travelers before us, we have had the chance to visit some exotic places and learn some important new things. We've met people from other times, cultures, and disciplines, as well as superheros from the pages of comic books. We've seen amazing feats of skill, strength, daring, and kindness. We've discovered the power of a promise, the magic of a conversation, and the wonder of a new and very different performance. We've also witnessed people who have to be brilliant 24/7, others who are committed to solving any request, still others whose world provides no room for mistakes, and an odd cast of characters for whom nothing is everything. We've even wandered with amazing animals across a harsh and unforgiving terrain.

So what does this mean for all of us and the geniuses we work with—in companies and organizations that are large and small, new and old?

Think of yourself, your colleagues, and your company or organization as explorers in search of treasures or insight that will define a new and more compelling world of value for your customers. Hopefully, you now have a clearer appreciation for the genius that is all around you. With your eyes open to a world of possibilities, you'll be amazed at what you can discover.

In Part III, I'd like to give you a straightforward way to make these journeys and the many others that you and your colleagues will take in the days ahead not just a source of inspiration but a source of competitive advantage. I'd like to do it by getting you comfortable with your own life as a traveler whose genius will depend on finding your own song and working together with others in your organization to create a new and different symphony of customer value. It will also depend on redefining your definition of leaders and leadership and creating new opportunities for everyone to take the lead in making a difference.

Let's go back for a moment to the meeting that started it all when a group of very smart people sat around a table and struggled to come up with an "out-of-the-box" idea. Failing that, we set out on a series of journeys to bring genius into the room, and at each stop along the way we discovered some amazing people, animals, and ideas. Possibly one of them in particular resonates with you and your colleagues as you look at your company or organization and its potential to deliver compelling value to those you serve. Possibly you saw elements of genius at several of our stops along the way that could be combined into a new and more compelling approach to deliver greater value that really matters. Or possibly you now have a better understanding that genius is all around us, and you are eager to head out on an entirely different journey to find other different ideas that matter to your marketplace.

Think of these ideas you have just discovered as a simple challenge to become a lifelong traveler to places near and far and to become a lifelong learner who is committed to the never-ending task of unlocking value for the customers you choose to serve. Their needs refuse to stand still, and it is unlikely that your best competitors will stand by idly. So your curiosity and passion for delivering ever greater value must also keep moving ahead. Think of the iPod. Will it survive the "next great thing," or will its definition of personal entertainment be too narrow in a world of more versatile devices? Think of your quest for genius as an ongoing journey to unlock value.

We don't have to travel around the world to find genius, though visiting different places, people, and ideas would certainly be among the most powerful journeys we could take to change or enhance our perspectives as individuals, companies, and organizations. Great ideas and insights are literally around each and every corner. We can find them:

- In the halls of a great or even not-so-great museum;
- Along the banks of a quiet stream;
- In a great book or an award-winning movie;
- On advertisements posted on buses that pass by;
- At a street fair, parade, or festival honoring another culture;
- In comic books about other worlds beyond our imagination;.
- At a lecture held at a local university on a topic that has nothing to do with us;

- In a performance of any type—
    - A modern dance ensemble;
    - An opera;
    - A soccer match;
    - A circus; or
    - A school play.
- In conversations overheard on the bus or subway;.
- At a family reunion;
- At a playground where children are constantly inventing new games; or
- On the streets where the future of cultures is being invented.

Ideas and possibilities abound, so go out there and breathe them in. Explore. Ask questions. Dare to be curious and amazed at the genius around you. No matter where you and your organization call home, there is more than enough magic to inspire you without ever having to get on a plane.

Feel free to use the ten big ideas we learned together in our initial journeys as the starting point on your travels. Think about the implications of each for creating greater customer success. In some ways, all of our companies and organizations would benefit from being better at all of the ideas presented here, but we can't do everything. The specific needs of our customers should dictate where we start and which ideas provide the best starting point for reinventing the world of our business. Use these needs as the basis for your strategy to deliver more compelling value. Commit as a team to take your own journey of discovery in unlocking the full potential of the idea.

And here's a bit more guidance on how to get it done . . .

chapter Fifteen

Unlocking the Genius Within

Or...
How to find the brilliance in ourselves...

I love to sing and have a great fascination with singing as an activity and as a concept. In fact, I find myself singing spontaneously a lot of the time and even stop at a moment of inspiration to compose serious or silly songs. Fortunately for our customers, I have rarely started singing at a meeting. I laugh a lot instead and mostly for the right reasons. I tend to sing when I'm not working. I sing a lot in the car, which sometimes earns me the praise of our kids, but more often than not they think I'm crazy. "Papa's lost it now!" is a common refrain.

During speeches and seminars, I routinely ask large groups of adults how many of them are very good singers, and you might not be surprised to find out that only a small percentage of people raise their hands. In fact, over the past seven years of asking this question to thousands of grownups, the figure is roughly 2 percent.

Then I ask people to pretend that they are young children about to enter school for the first time. "Now, kids," I inquire, "how many of you are really good singers?" After a momentary pause, most people get with the program and realize they should raise their hands, or, more accurately, that they should raise their hands enthusiastically. "That's better," I reply, demonstrating the rousing response given by your average class of kindergarteners.

> In order to become the explorer that you need to be, you must figure out the song in you and how to bring it out in all of its glory.

I then point out that somewhere between childhood and adulthood, roughly 98 percent of grownups (by my less-than-scientific survey) have lost the ability to sing! And it probably starts not long after we arrive in school when someone tells us that we either have a bad voice or are singing a stupid song.

"Are small children great singers?" I continue. Their response is a resounding "No!" But I certainly don't agree, and I don't let people off the hook so easily. Maybe not by the standards of Placido Domingo, Ella Fitzgerald, Sara Brightman, Johnny Mathis, or Five for Fighting, but by the standard that matters most, which is their own small children are fantastic singers. (And by the current standard of what's on MTV, they are absolutely brilliant singers.)

Singing comes naturally to humans. We are actually physically designed to sing—not necessarily to sing opera or to imitate the Temptations or other great Motown groups—but to sing with joy and conviction. It feels very good to sing. Admit it. If it didn't, most of you would not be singing in the shower, or in your car when you are driving alone, or on a quiet walk in the woods.

Singing, it turns out, is one of the few things that has occurred in practically every culture and civilization on our planet, with the possible exception of those cultures whose members have taken a vow of silence (and with all due respect, I would imagine that their members still sing to themselves when they are alone). And the list of universal cultural traits is not a particularly long one.

Find the Song in You

This leads us to an essential idea. In every one of us there is a wonderful and compelling song waiting to be sung. But it is a song that is rarely expressed to its full potential, and with the passage of time it is harder to bring out. Yet I would argue that in order to become the explorer that you need to be, you must figure out the song in you and how to bring it out in all of its glory. That means finding the place where you can make a compelling difference.

So think about what inspires you to make a difference. If that's too tough a question to start out with, think about what once inspired you to be the best you could possibly be. What really matters to you? Where do you fit into a picture of delivering compelling value to customers? What ideas have we unlocked on our journeys that might lead you to become more engaged, curious, innovative, and brilliant? Who could you relate to? What journey or journeys struck a chord in you? Or would you rather set out on

Think about what inspires you to make a difference. Begin with the belief that you can make a compelling difference.

your own to find a different song to sing? The funny thing is that for many people their song and the way that they deliver compelling value often have little to do with their job description.

Then begin with the belief that you can make a compelling difference. All you need is the right insight and the right circumstances. You'll have to stretch a bit, which means broadening your knowledge of yourself, the customers you serve, and the limits of your own imagination.

For a while I have had the unusual habit of looking in our customers' "in boxes" to see what they read, where they hang out, and who and what is on their radar screens. I typically find cause for concern and real insight on why there is a lack of genius and creativity in so many companies and organizations. Most people spend their few free minutes a day reading stuff that doesn't really matter. Or, I should clarify, doesn't really matter if we are trying to provide different and compelling value as individuals and organizations. This stuff is typically about their own industries or their specific fields of expertise. So people in an information technology company tend to read magazines, journals, and blogs about IT, and they tend to get invitations to meetings and conferences about IT. The folks in the finance department tend to read magazines, journals, and blogs about finance or, more specifically, finance for IT finance professionals. Talk about corporate and functional in-breeding. The good news is that everyone else in your industry or your functional area is reading, hearing, and learning the same things. So if you are really good at keeping on top of this stuff, you can be just as good as your best colleagues and competitors in other companies who are all keeping on top of the very same stuff.

Maybe we should be focusing our research on a much broader form of curiosity.

Or you can look at very different things.

As leading pharmaceutical companies struggle to discover the next generation of blockbuster drugs, most of their people are reading the same scientific journals, attending the same meetings, and talking about the latest insights from the very same science. After all, they have made multibillion dollar investments in brilliant researchers, world-class laboratories, and information technology that enables them to slice through data and possible compounds faster and more efficiently than ever before. But this research model is producing fewer and fewer breakthroughs while at the same time the lives of more and more people depend on their genius.

So a few enlightened ones are actually taking journeys to places filled with very different inspiration and insight. Everyday geniuses in companies like Novartis are now traveling around the world and back in time to explore the possibilities of ancient remedies in countries like China. Maybe there are lessons to be learned from herbs, treatments, and acupuncture that we will never discover in the finest labs. Maybe there are equally important lessons

Make it part of your routine to discover compelling ideas from other industries and other walks of life.

about diet, meditation, and exercise that hold some of the keys to success. Maybe there is an even more compelling lesson to be learned in the combination of ideas from different places and different domains. A drug, an herb, some yoga, and regular participation in the Friskis&Svettis fitness program might be the essential cure for what ails so many of us. Maybe the adage "better life through chemistry" has kept us from seeing the real answer. Maybe the right combination of ancient wisdom and modern technology is the right approach. Maybe we should be focusing our research on a much broader form of curiosity.

And maybe you should be, too. Da Vinci didn't talk to humans about how to fly because they had no idea how to do it. He wandered around and looked at birds. It would take several more centuries for it to happen, but it wasn't for a lack of thinking differently about the world and the magic of flight.

What are you most curious about? Inside that curiosity exists the beginning of an amazing song.

Turn Your Curiosity into Action

Put yourself in the middle of different ideas and ways of thinking. Read everything you can that is different and in its own way compelling. Go to seminars and conferences where they talk about different stuff that matters to different people. Listen, watch, and expose yourself to as many new ideas as possible as the best way to get your creativity flowing. Make it part of your routine to discover compelling ideas from other industries and other walks of life. Then try to set aside time each day, or at least each week, to look for new ideas that could, with the proper tinkering, deliver compelling value for the customers you serve. The more ideas you unlock, the more likely you are to make a powerful connection between new and different thinking and the important needs of your customers. You might have to put ideas together that don't on the face of it seem to belong together in order to unlock unique value.

The more ideas you unlock, the more likely you are to make a powerful connection between new and different thinking and the important needs of your customers.

If you need a bit more help getting comfortable with your own amazing potential to explore, think, and create, here are six things you can do today to strengthen your ability and genius:

Expand Your Reading Horizons.

Subscribe to and read enthusiastically at least three magazines or journals that interest you, and focus on new ideas that have nothing to do with your company, organization, or job. Then start to broaden the array of books and other sources of information and inspiration you expose yourself to. You might also want to make regular visits to your favorite bookstore or library to see what ideas are hot and promising.

Hit the Road in Search of New Ideas.

Take mini-excursions into the world around you to unlock fresh ideas and new ways of doing things. Create a mix of "planned activities," where you go to a specific place that is likely to offer real insight for a particular problem or opportunity, and "unplanned wanderings," where you go with the flow and keep your eyes wide open to any and all possibilities. Pay particular attention to all of the nothings that really seem to matter and all of the promises that are being made and kept. Look at signs and billboards along the way and pause to overhear other people's conversations.

Ask Stimulating Questions Whenever You Have the Chance.

Start asking more questions in every meeting you lead or are invited to attend. Try to challenge yourself and your colleagues in a positive way to question everything you are doing with the objective of determining whether there might be a better way. You might even ask people to think about what should be done to be perfect, faster,

Talk to strangers whose work and ideas fascinate you.

more responsive, or more remarkable. Or ask them to think about what it means to create the most compelling performance.

Become Your Customer's Best Student.

Hang out with your customers and commit to learning as much as you can about their world and the challenges they face. Then invite them on some of your journeys of discovery to explore and unlock new ideas and possibilities together. Create a new and more compelling conversation together that challenges both of you to anticipate their evolving needs and imagine a more compelling picture of their future success.

Make Friends with Unusual People.

Talk to strangers whose work and ideas fascinate you in order to understand how others use their curiosity and passion to deliver compelling value for those they choose to serve. Befriend people in businesses and organizations that you admire. Get to know artists who are constantly trying to stretch our thinking and do something different that matters. Get involved in organizations that are really making a difference in your community, especially ones that bring together people from many walks of life.

Pay particular attention to all of the nothings that really seem to matter and all of the promises that are being made and kept.

Tutor a child who will also mentor you on how they see the world. Commit to building the best and most diverse network possible. Nurturing relationships with people who have different interests, perspectives, and ways of thinking about things that matter to them is a great way to keep your own thinking fresh and relevant.

Cast an Even Wider Net.

Look to nature, history, geography, and the genius of other people and other cultures as an untapped source of great inspiration. Dare yourself to understand what other people *and* other cultures know so clearly and how it might apply to your world and the world of your customers.

By doing each of these things, you are likely to strengthen your ability to deliver greater genius to your customers and discover the real song that lives inside you. Then remember that the greatest skill anyone possesses is a sense of curiosity and possibilities. This skill is heightened when applied to things that interest you and really matter. And stop saying that you are not curious and creative.

The greatest skill anyone possesses is a sense of curiosity and possibilities.

Like the ability to sing, these are gifts that you and all of the geniuses in your company or organization were born with. So now is your chance to dust them off and put them to great use!

chapter Sixteen

Bringing Genius to Scale

Or . . .
How to create an organization that nurtures
the genius in all of its people. . .

Now let's put all of your genius together to create the amazing music that will deliver truly compelling value for the customers you choose to serve. To do this, you will have to align your individual song, or at least your potential to sing, with a clear understanding of why your company or organization exists and what is required for it to be brilliant. Then you will need to take a different look at the fundamental assets of your organization, i.e., your colleagues and their unique talents, which include the very human abilities to be curious, passionate, and collaborative in meeting the needs of customers.

Let me start by suggesting the essential steps in a straightforward framework.

Create a Clear, Compelling, and Shared Purpose
I'm going to make a bold assumption: your company or organization exists for a reason that matters to the customers you choose

to serve. Otherwise it probably would have disappeared, like the dinosaurs and the woolly mammoths. But before you decide to pat yourselves on the collective back, let me ask a tough question. Is your purpose as an organization clear, compelling, and shared by all of the geniuses (or potential geniuses) you work with? If recent research and my experience with more than 300 companies and organizations is any indication, the answer is a resounding "probably not." So if you answered "yes," you and your organization have a distinct advantage over most of your competitors in bringing genius to scale. Not that you should let it go to your head.

Having a clear, compelling, and shared sense of purpose—a reason to exist that really matters— is the minimum daily requirement for unlocking the genius in your organization.

I'm not going to get into the debate about the importance of vision, as much as I believe it is vital to the long-term viability of any individual or organization. I have seen too many companies create "vision statements" that are clever and meaningless just to check off the "vision" box on their to-do lists. However, I would like to suggest that you visit the excellent work on vision by Jim Collins and his colleagues. But I am going to suggest that having a clear, compelling, and shared sense of purpose—a reason to exist that really matters—is the minimum daily requirement for unlocking the genius in your organization and all of its people. When the purpose is clear, compelling, and shared, it becomes much easier to engage people and unlock their genius for the simple reason that everyone knows what target they are being asked to hit and why. And everyone has a clearer picture of the types of ideas and innovations that are most likely to deliver compelling value to customers. Then they are free to explore the world in search of big and small things that are likely to really matter.

This clarity of purpose is a big part of the reason why Toyota, one of the world's most focused and successful companies, reports that of the 2 million employee suggestions it receives in a year about 85 percent are implemented. Their people, it seems, understand the company's purpose and the types of ideas that will help to achieve it. Most companies and organizations, however, are not so skillful or lucky. So make an honest assessment of whether you and your colleagues are all on the same page. Don't let Toyota's size and great success deter you. They weren't always as big or brilliant as they are today.

A number of years ago, I had the rare opportunity to help unlock the genius in all 460 employees of a biotechnology supply company. It was a wonderful assignment or "experiment" and one that you can actually do in your company or organization.

We began by thinking about the company's customers and what really mattered to them. They were, for the most part, leading and emerging biotechnology and pharmaceutical companies that were trying to create and commercialize breakthrough therapies to save or improve people lives. Success in their world, as one senior research scientist put it, "was tougher than finding a needle in a haystack." And with the high

Everyone could become the "entrepreneurs" of their own jobs—by taking initiative and seeking opportunities to unlock greater value.

cost of development, the clock was always ticking. Their focus on the value of human life was definitely clear and compelling. *But so was the supply company's focus.* As one of the most highly regarded manufacturers of cell culture media and other products essential to biological research and drug discovery, they were a critical link in the process. Their products had to live up to the highest quality standards and be available when customers needed them. They also had to support their products with the right knowledge and responsiveness. This required creating a new, more compelling notion of what it meant to be a partner who was continuously raising the bar in terms of the value it delivered.

As you might imagine, everyone had an important role to play—whether they were in product development, quality assurance, production, distribution, customer and technical support, marketing, sales, finance, or any other function. The customers' needs drove their sense of purpose, and that purpose provided the essential focus for individual and collective action. Now all that was needed, we believed, was the right challenge to bring out the genius in all of their people.

That challenge was leadership's commitment to become even better at delivering value to the customers and enabling them to be even more successful in their difficult work. This meant being faster, more responsive, and more skillful in helping customers to maximize the value of their products, services, and solutions. But instead of mandates on how it would be done, the leadership team began with the simple notion that each and every employee in the organization could make a real difference in the lives of the customers if given the guidance and support to do so. In essence, that everyone could become the "entrepreneurs" of their own jobs—by taking initiative and seeking opportunities to unlock greater value.

Product design, process, and execution are critical.

To do this, we got everyone together, rolled up our sleeves, and taught them how to step out of their comfort zone and look at their roles with a sense of curiosity and openness. As part of this, we showed them how to leave the building in search of fresh ideas from other companies, industries, organizations, and other parts of their own lives, including social and civic involvement, hobbies and recreation, family and friends, and even shopping. We asked them to forget about how they were doing things today and to imagine the best possible way to serve their outside or internal customers. Not surprisingly, they started wandering around together in search of clues and insight. Within thirty days, more than 200 important changes were suggested.

> **There is magic in the big and little details of our dealings with customers and that magic can be the most compelling thing.**

Then we taught everyone how to develop action plans for evaluating their most promising ideas, how to test them with customers, and how to make the right ones happen. In the following ninety days, 75 percent of these ideas were implemented to improve the customer experience and support greater customer success—changes that resulted in faster production and distribution, fewer defects, more timely resolution of problems, enhanced "knowledge" support, reduced cost, the start of two entirely new product lines, enhanced collaboration internally, and greater overall customer satisfaction.

Understanding your customers' world, what matters most to them, what they hope to accomplish in their wildest dreams of success, and your potential role in making it happen frames the essential first step in bringing genius to scale. It is a step that you cannot succeed without. Ignore it and you might as well close up shop and go home because you and your colleagues will have little or no chance to compete. And you will likely frustrate the heck out of anyone in your organization who wants to make a difference. Get it right and you and the geniuses you work with can head out in search of compelling value.

So take a few minutes to ask the following questions: What is your real purpose as a company or organization? Is your purpose clear, compelling, and shared by everyone? Is it driven by a real understanding of what your customers are trying to accomplish and what really matters to them? Are you and your colleagues passionate about doing whatever it takes to deliver the greatest value to the customers you choose to serve? If you answer "yes" to each of these questions, you have solved the first part of what is required to bring genius to scale. Now you can turn your attention to the notion of creating value that matters.

Unlock and Deliver Compelling Value

On our ten journeys, we traveled the world in search of compelling value and found it in a wide range of places. Now your job is to connect that learning with the real needs of your customers and to take your own journeys to either reinforce what you have already learned or come up with even better models for achieving greater customer success. So think about which ideas provide the best starting point for your company or organization.

Is Perfection Important?

Let's start by revisiting the two boldest ideas we discovered—the notion of providing an unconditional guarantee of satisfaction and the idea that anything short of perfection is not an option. Remember L.L. Bean, the guy with bad feet who, upon screwing up, made a solemn pledge to his customers to provide a product that would stand up to their highest standard of value? Or the team working on the Atlas 5 rocket (that only got paid for each mission success)? We learned from each that product design, process, and execution are critical. We also learned that understanding what mattered most to the customer was the essential starting point in figuring out how to meet their needs and expectations perfectly.

But this begs the question of whether your customers expect or desire perfection

Time and expertise matters.

and how easy it is to make it happen in your business. After all, if you could figure out the "perfect" customer experience and achieve it, you would be very hard to beat. In fact, if you could come close to delivering perfection and could honestly and skillfully address any situations in which you missed the mark, you would be very hard to beat. So try to use these ideas as a starting point for building the most perfect customer experience possible, given the realities of your world. Then figure out how to change those realities to reinvent the notion of value in your industry.

Or Are the Nature and Details of Your Performance?

But what if other things matter even more than perfection? Remember *Cirque du Soleil,* the band of street performers who ended up reinventing the 2,500-year-old institution of the circus? Or *Seinfeld,* the television show that won praise for making fun of our shared experience as humans whose lives are filled with fears, flaws, and phobias? They showed us that there is magic in the big and little details of our dealings with customers and that magic can be the most compelling thing. So think about the nature and details of the performance that is your business and whether you can make it as compelling and filled with wonder as possible. But don't just think about a dramatic conclusion where value is revealed. Picture the entire performance from before it starts until after it is done and how you can sweep the customers off their feet.

Then think about all of the little and big things or "moments of truth," as Jan Carlson the former CEO of SAS

Airlines once called them, that are truly critical interactions in the customer experience your organization delivers. Begin by focusing on the ones that seem to matter most to the customer, then commit to figuring out how to make each one remarkable. Again, applying these ideas to your organization and working out the details could be truly compelling.

Or Are Speed, Commitment, and the Right Skill at Any Time?

Maybe speed and bringing the right knowledge, commitment, and skill to bear 24/7 are essential in your marketplace. Remember the beautiful, designed-for-speed cat that accelerated faster from a standing start than an expensive sports car? Or the amazing shock trauma center where they literally brought people back from the edge of death after suffering critical injuries? Or the highly attentive team of problem-solvers at the Ritz-Carlton on Central Park? These journeys showed us that time and expertise matters. There is reason to believe that this combination will become a more important determinant of business success in a world that never stops. So think about those

Challenge yourself and your organization to be a world-class provider of thoughtful and amazing relationships.

situations in which speed and just the right knowledge are critical to your customer's success and figure out exactly what it takes to be brilliant in making each happen. Do you need faster people, faster communication, faster problem-diagnosis and problem-solving abilities, different talents, a better network or Rolodex, better skill at sharing knowledge and turning it to action, more inspiration and real passion for solving problems or creating opportunities, or simply a better design for how you and the geniuses you work with get things done?

If speed, commitment, and highly specialized skill matters most to your customers, challenge yourself and your organization to be the most inspired, compelling provider of these in your world.

Is a Reason to Smile Important?

What if there is an entirely different level of value that your customers are seeking or would appreciate? What if they long to have more meaningful conversations or a greater sense of joy from the companies and organizations that they choose to serve them? Think back to our walk through the neighborhood with a nine-year-old Girl Scout who could put most professional salespeople to shame. Or revisit our Friskis&Svettis morning class along the North Sea with thirty-five regular people who actually seemed to enjoy exercising. Then imagine the types of compelling conversations that you and your company or organization could have on a regular basis with your customers. Conversations that really mattered about things near and dear to their hearts. Imagine what would happen if you could do things that made your customer healthier and more capable of doing what mattered most to them.

If real conversations and the promise of a smile matter most to your customers, challenge yourself and your organization to be a world-class provider of thoughtful and amazing relationships. Make the ideas we unlocked on these two journeys a starting point for your commitment to deliver compelling value.

Or Is the Ability to Anticipate the Future?
Which leads us back to our final journey...

No matter who our customers are, we can assume that their world is getting more and more complex. The challenges they face, or will face, are likely to be bigger and more difficult than before. They run the risk of being blindsided by things they did not see coming—unless we commit to helping them avoid danger or seize a new opportunity. Remember our comic-book hero Spider-Man in the awesome spandex costume? He was given an amazing gift through the unfortunate bite of a spider. Among his other superpowers, Peter Parker gained the ability to anticipate danger. Yet, as improbable as it sounds, it is a gift that all of us share if we work together as focused and passionate organizations. We have the remarkable ability to put our collective ears to the ground or minds to the future and help our customers avoid danger or make great things happen. This skill should be part of all of our formulas for delivering compelling value. It is one journey that can enable us to bring our collective genius front and center.

Build a Culture of Curiosity and Commitment

Not long ago, I was asked to provide guidance to a prominent research company that was stuck in its efforts to spark innovation. They had, like many of their peers, created a program to encourage new ideas that featured a "suggestion box" as a way to spur the best thinking of their people coupled with modest financial incentives for the would-be innovators. They hoped that this initiative, with its promise that "no idea is stupid," would lead to some brilliant recommendations.

Instead they got a predictable assortment of suggestions that were all over the map. To be fair, there were some reasonable ideas for improving internal operations. There were interesting ideas for making the work environment more hospitable. There were straightforward ideas for tweaking some existing offerings that had lost their appeal. There were grand ideas for getting into entirely new lines of businesses, and there were half-baked ideas for reinventing the core business in ways that might not matter to the customers they served. But there were few ideas that had any real potential for changing the game in a way that really mattered to customers. When they asked me what I thought had gone wrong, I had to work hard to fight back the tears.

While no ideas are stupid, some ideas are smarter than others especially when "smart" has a direct connection to what matters most to the customers we choose to serve. But their program gave no clear guidance on who the customers actually were and

We have the remarkable ability to put our collective ears to the ground or minds to the future and help our customers avoid danger or make great things happen.

what they were trying to accomplish. In fact, it didn't even put the customer at the center of efforts to innovate. Its broad call for ideas "that would improve the business" was not unlike a particular late-night television show's call for people to perform "stupid human tricks." While it might uncover some amazing (and random) talents or business ideas, it was not likely to generate possibilities that had the potential to matter.

If we are simply seeking amusement, or trying to appease people frustrated by our lack of innovation, a broadly framed suggestion program is an okay strategy. But if we are serious about customer and business success, it is not. Remember, all of our companies and organizations are trying to compete in a harsh and unforgiving world. It's eat or be eaten—deliver value or become irrelevant. We need ideas that matter, and if they also happen to be amusing, that's icing on the proverbial cake. So, as we emphasized earlier, we need to give people the clearest possible "customer-centric" guidance. We need to ask questions that help us to understand not only what matters to the customer today but also what might be possible for them tomorrow and beyond.

That's not all. We also need to build a culture of curiosity and commitment in which people understand and are willing to do the hard work required to make any important idea happen.

It's eat or be eaten— deliver value or become irrelevant.

We can't afford to create a process for suggesting ideas that is too easy for those who have the power to make a real difference. But in their case, there was very little required of a would-be innovator. There was no requirement to question the basic assumptions about the way the world currently worked and how it might be changed to create greater customer success. There were no required journeys of discovery to spark fresh thinking. There were no required demonstrations of passion and commitment to a recommended idea. There were no requirements to envision how a team of everyday geniuses might work together to make the idea happen. Just make a suggestion—on our simple form, the back of an envelope, or the placemat from a local restaurant.

If only delivering greater customer value was that simple.

While inspiration is everywhere, it is simply the starting point. Making a meaningful idea happen takes effort. Edison had a great idea to create a light bulb, but it took him 1,000 tries to get it right. The Wright Brothers were convinced that humans could fly like birds, but they swallowed a lot of sand before their plane ever took flight at Kitty Hawk. Hyundai made a lot of mediocre cars before they figured out how to work together to make a high-quality vehicle. The founders of Cirque du Soleil tested their ideas on a lot of street corners before they created a formula to conquer the world of entertainment. They are part of an unending list of geniuses that all of us must aspire to join. Don't we believe that we ought to do some homework, too?

Remember the guidance that Spider-Man received from his uncle: "With great power there must also come great responsibility." We all have the power to create compelling ideas, but with that power we must also challenge each other to take our great responsibility for delivering compelling value seriously. We must work together to build a culture that asks us to imagine, explore, question, refine, collaborate, and then bring brilliant ideas to market. We must work together to build a culture that inspires us to see the back of our envelopes as the start of our journeys, not as the final destination. We must commit our efforts, talents, and passion to the noble cause of achieving greater customer success.

Connect Your Assets to the Value You Seek to Deliver

When does a simple song become a symphony? Is it when the right people and the right talents come together with an overriding commitment to make something important happen? Is it when everyone knows their part and its relationship to the whole? Is it when we've practiced so that it can be performed flawlessly? Or is it when the singers are excited that their part brings out the magic in them and everyone else? It is all of these things. It is a celebration of the individual passions and collective assets or talents that we possess as companies and organizations.

While inspiration is everywhere, it is simply the starting point. Making a meaningful idea happen takes effort.

Underlying the discussion throughout this book is the simple notion, outlined early on, that everyone in your company or organization has a unique set of talents, gifts, and potential capabilities that can make a difference in the lives of the customers you serve. Some of these talents are obvious, such as a particular technical ability or a certain type of knowledge. Other talents and gifts are less likely to appear on their company bio or resume, such as:

- An amazing level of energy and enthusiasm;
- A real sense of curiosity and openness;
- The ability to see possibilities that others do not see;
- A deep understanding of other industries, cultures, and disciplines;
- Skill at communicating or interacting with others;
- The ability to make things happen;
- The ability to overcome insurmountable obstacles;
- A gift for remaining calm and focused under stress;
- The ability to solve complicated problems;
- The gift of experience and having been there before;
- The gift of having made important mistakes and learned from them; and
- The ability to see the future.

These skills and gifts, among others, and the diversity of people and perspectives that bring them are the real assets of your company or organization. However, they are rarely utilized to their full potential.

If you really want to bring genius to scale, you and your company or organization must commit to thinking very differently about all of the uniquely human assets that arrive at work each day and how they can be leveraged to delivering compelling value. You have to commit to looking everyone in the eye and the heart to figure out all of the songs in them and all of the talents they could bring to bear to do things that matter. You have to hold a lot of auditions until people discover their real song and the powerful connection between their song and the songs of others.

Then you need to map those songs or assets to the picture of what you are trying to accomplish in ways that inspire people to be brilliant. Unleash them on journeys of discovery to unlock the details of your formula for delivering value.

Reward Explorers in Ways That Matter

We have set a clear, compelling, and shared purpose to guide us. We have journeyed in search of value that will enable us to lay claim to that purpose better than anyone else. We have assembled a team with skills, gifts, songs, and a few warts who are eager and ready to make great things happen. We have committed to figuring out how to make this cast of characters work together to deliver the most compelling value possible for the customers we choose to serve. So what's left in our formula for bringing genius to scale?

Rewards that matter. After all the research that has been done on this topic, it is increasingly clear that the only rewards that get results are the ones that matter to the people we are counting on to do brilliant things. These rewards are likely to be as different as the people themselves and just as likely to say more about the chance to make a difference than the chance to make a financial windfall.

So don't start with the rewards in the hope that they will inspire individual and collective genius. Start with the individual and collective geniuses and ask them what

The only rewards that get results are the ones that matter to the people we are counting on to do brilliant things.

it will take to get them to do something that really matters. Then be open to answers that might surprise you. In fact, few discoveries occur because someone is on a quest to get rich quickly. Most occur because an individual or a team wants to make a real difference. If this is the case, the greatest rewards are the ones that make it possible for them to actually do brilliant things—rewards that give them the freedom, tools, resources, and support to try something new and to push the limits of what is possible in the hope that their efforts will see the light of day, rewards that enable mere mortals to unlock the genius in themselves, each other, and their organizations.

The one remaining piece is the role that a new brand of leader must play in making your symphony of genius and possibility come alive.

chapter seventeen

The Essential Work of Leaders

Or ...
How to become a compelling leader in the brave new world of customer and business success...

What is the essential work of leaders, and how should our understanding of leadership change in a world that demands that our companies and organizations consistently create compelling value for those we choose to serve?

It's a big question but one with a relatively simple answer. So with all due respect to the many brilliant and thoughtful leaders, academics, and consultants who have written great and lengthy works on the subject of leadership, let me use one more short journey from a different but familiar walk of life to demonstrate what I mean.

The Magic of a Great Children's Book

Picture the scene in a first-grade classroom at story time. It could be a scene from your own childhood, from the world of your children, grandchildren, nieces, or nephews or from a classroom in the community where you live or work. It could also be a scene from a school halfway around the world, as there is something universal about reading or telling stories. Whatever the case, the scene is all about the wonder of stories, the magic of childhood, and the most important work of leaders.

Now imagine that all of the students have found their places on the carpet in the corner of the classroom and the teacher has taken her seat in the special reading chair. She has called everyone to attention and announced with a giant smile that today's book is *Where the Wild Things Are* by Maurice Sendak. Winner of the 1964 Caldecott Medal for best picture book, this delightful tale with its compelling message and wonderful illustrations should probably be required reading (or re-reading) for anyone in a company or organization.

In the story, a mischievous boy named Max puts on his wolf suit and tries one too many pranks to the great displeasure of his mother. She, in turn, calls him "Wild Thing" and sends him off to his room without supper. Once in his room, Max's imagination takes flight. First a forest appears and grows into a dense jungle of possibilities. Then a small boat arrives to take Max off to a land where the wildest of creatures live—creatures intent on scaring the wits out of him.

Leaders are the ones who capture everyone's attention and spark a sense of curiosity by opening a book to a world where ideas, questions, and possibilities can take flight.

But Max scares the Wild Things instead by "staring into all their yellow eyes without blinking once" and becomes the ruler of this dark and magical place. When Max commands, "Let the wild rumpus start!" great merriment ensues, until he realizes (like so many characters before him) that he really misses home—and he sends the Wild Things off to bed without their supper.

I'll leave you and your colleagues to read the rest of the story, which I hope you will do together, because we've read enough in these few moments to unlock the essential work of leaders.

Needless to say, the clever and compelling story, along with the delightful and captivating illustrations, has grabbed the attention of everyone in the room. When the teacher asks if anyone can relate to Max, his emotions, and his unusual journey, all hands shoot up with their own tales to tell. "I once got lost in a forest filled with scary creatures," one child exclaims. "Me, too," another adds. Then a lively discussion follows about getting mad, needing some alone time, conquering the things that scare us, missing our family, and letting our imaginations run wild. A host of additional questions and answers follow. After each idea or question, the teacher makes a point of thanking the students for their contribution.

When we can't find our place, leaders help us to discover the song within us and its relationship to the symphony or performance we are trying to create.

You are probably asking, "But what does this have to do with leadership?"

Leaders Are the Ones Who Start a Story That Matters

Leaders are the ones who capture everyone's attention and spark a sense of curiosity by opening a book to a world where ideas, questions, and possibilities can take flight. They transform our purpose into the beginning of a living and vivid story about what we can become, and they ask essential questions that challenge each of us to find our place as the story starts to unfold. They ask us to find a place in which we can create compelling value for ourselves, our companies and organizations, and those we choose to serve. And when we can't find our place, leaders help us to discover the song within us and its relationship to the symphony or performance we are trying to create.

Leaders are the ones who realize that in order to deliver compelling value many people will have to take turns in the lead.

Although the best leaders are skilled at starting the story and framing the picture of what is possible, they need not read every line. They are also skilled at asking questions that challenge us to begin a process of inquiry into what our companies and organizations can become. But they need not ask every question. Once we get started, their essential role is to keep the conversation going and compel us to be engaged and questioning conspirators. Our quest is to unlock the greatest potential value for our customers by allowing our innate creativity and imagination to take flight. Leaders are the ones who realize that in order to deliver compelling value many people will have to take turns in the lead.

Leaders refuse to allow us to take "no" or "yes" for an answer until we have become part of the journey and actively explored a world of possibilities, and then they refuse to let us off the hook until we commit to creating something of value.

Leaders Maintain Focus on Delivering Value That Matters

As the journey unfolds, leaders are the ones who make sure that our focus remains clearly on the real needs of the customers we choose to serve and what it takes to change the game in a way that delivers compelling value. They inspire us to believe that anything is possible if we have the vision and commitment to make it happen.

Leaders resist the pull to be cautious, slightly different, or just a bit better. They ask us to make no small plans in meeting the customers' expectations, hopes, and wildest dreams, unless those initial steps along the wing are designed to help us get our bearings for the real flight that follows.

Leaders hold the lamp that lights our way on the journey to what we can and must become.

Leaders create a culture of exploration in which everyone seeks to discover and unlock compelling value. Leaders are the ones who help us understand how to be curious, open, and brilliant together.

Leaders Acknowledge Every Contribution

Leaders are also the ones who acknowledge everyone's contribution, no matter how big or small, and thank everyone for being engaged. In doing so, they encourage even greater participation and challenge us to stretch beyond our comfort zones to discover the genius in us and connect it with the genius all around us.

Leaders hold the lamp that lights our way on the journey to what we can and must become.

Concluding Note

Customers matter more than anything else. They alone are the reason why companies, nonprofit organizations, and governments—in democracies, at least—exist. To remain relevant to the customers you choose to serve, you must be committed to understanding their evolving needs and to continually delivering unique value that matters. You will never do this if you are content with incremental change or merely copying the best practices of your best competitors. To improve, you will need to regularly reinvent the game that you and your company or organization chooses to play. And the best way to do this is to unlock the genius of all your people so they can unlock a world filled with compelling ideas that, once adapted, will truly matter to your customers.

Ideas abound in the most expected places and the most unusual places. In this book, I have shared ten of my favorite ones, but they are only a starting point for your own journeys and exploration. Whatever you and your company or organization do, seek to discover the best insight and apply it with skill and passion to your world. Unlike Marco Polo, it won't take you three years to get to China or anywhere else. A wealth of possibilities is a short hop away or literally at your fingertips. The world, with its diversity of people, thinking, and creations, has come to us. It is here to be experienced, understood, and applied. So breathe in the possibilities.

You and the other geniuses around you have the power to create your customers' greatest success and, in the process, the power to assure the future success of your own companies and organizations. It is a future that will belong to the curious. Your challenge is to be ready when the right ideas or possibilities present themselves and to be open to possibilities and curious about what they might mean when adapted to your company or organization's particular world and circumstances.

So dare to wake up tomorrow with your eyes wide open. To look around every corner. To talk with strangers. To ask a million questions and discover 10 million answers. Dare to find the song within you and to sing it aloud in the company of friends. Dare to find your place in the symphony of value that your company or organization can deliver. Dare to be compellingly different in the work and life you choose.

I said at the outset that the ideas contained in this book would level the playing field in any business or industry. Even the companies or organizations that were losing could become winners in a new world order driven by equal access to virtually unlimited sources of inspiration. I feel compelled to return to this thought before sending you on your way.

Obviously you have a far better chance to win in the future if you have been doing the right things up until now. Knowing your customers, meeting their needs, and delivering products, services, or solutions that matter today provide a much better starting position as the world spins faster and faster. But, quite simply, it is not enough. Customer loyalty merely buys you a ticket to deliver greater value tomorrow. As a result, even companies that have been doing poorly have a chance to reinvent themselves and change the game before our very eyes. It won't be easy, but it is not impossible to rise from the near dead. As we learned from the remarkable doctors and nurses at the shock trauma center, this could be your "golden hour," when the future of your company or organization hangs in the balance. Each of us has a chance to win, but the clock is ticking faster than we could have ever imagined. If there was ever a time to look at the world in a very different way, it is now.

With these final thoughts, I wish each and every one of you a safe and successful journey. Don't expect me to wish you "good luck!" because I don't think you will need it. There are more than enough great ideas for you and your colleagues to discover. And besides, I've known for a long time that I was surrounded by geniuses. Hopefully, I've convinced you that you are as well.

So let the fun and the magic begin!

Map of the Known World

If you'd like to test your knowledge of geography and a world filled with ideas, try to find the places we traveled to in the book on a map of the world or a globe. And while you're at it, see if you can find some new places with insight to share.

- White Men Swimming Slowly—England, South America, Australia, Solomon Islands
- Marco Polo's travels—the Silk Road from Italy to China
- Velcro®—The Alps
- Enterprise Rent-a-Car—St. Louis, Missouri
- Hertz—Chicago, Illinois
- Avis—Detroit, Michigan
- Apple—Silicon Valley, California
- Whole Foods Market—Austin, Texas
- L.L. Bean—Freeport, Maine
- Structural Systems—Thurmont, Maryland
- Girl Scouts—Neighborhoods throughout the world
- Starbucks—Seattle, Washington, and around the world
- Coffee houses—Baghdad, Tehran, London
- Cirque du Soleil—Quebec, Canada, and Sydney, Australia
- Ritz-Carlton New York—Central Park, New York City

- University of Maryland Shock Trauma Center—Baltimore, Maryland
- Cheetahs—Tanzania, Africa
- Seinfeld apartment—New York City
- Rocket science—Denver, Colorado, Cape Canaveral, and on to Jupiter and Pluto
- Friskis and Svettis—Bovallstrand, Sweden
- Spider-Man—New York City
- Hyundai—Seoul, South Korea; and
- Toyota—Aichi, Japan.
- Sony—Tokyo
- National Building Museum—Washington, D.C.
- Pit crews—racetracks around the world

Acknowledgments

O ne of the greatest pleasures in a project like this is the opportunity to thank everyone whose ideas and insight have helped to shape my thinking.

To all of our customers at VENTURE WORKS, I am honored to have had the chance to partner with you in exploring, learning, and attempting to deliver compelling value to the customers you choose to serve. You are proof that I have been surrounded by geniuses. Special thanks to Ken Allen, David Anderson, C.E. Andrews, Karen Blair, Cheryl Campbell, Jeff Cleveland, Mac Curtis, Paul DiPiazza, Bryan Even, David Forman, Ellen Glover, Bruce Gordon, Mike Hopp, Sudhakar Kesevan, Betsy Lee, Mary Frances Le Mat, Paul Lombardi, Jim Lynch, Jim McGinty, Donna Morea, Al Nahal, Eric Oetjen, Bill Piatt, Vic Pfeiffer, Beverly Robertson, Steve Robins, Zaki Saleh, George Schindler, Adam Sherer, Mike Smith, Matt Swayhoover, Charbel Tagher, Gary Taylor, Leif Ulstrup, Luis Vasquez-Ajmac, Gena Wade, and John Wasson.

Very special thanks to Marriott International for giving me the opportunity to test many of my ideas in a program designed for general managers of their hotels around the world. The chance to work with so many talented people from so many countries and cultures has been a wonderful gift. I'd particularly like to thank Ibrahim "I.B." Barghout in Dubai, Alexandre Esmeraldo in Costa Rica, John Northen in Shanghai, John Toti in Curacao, Mike Stengel in New York, Patrick Franssen in Florida, Mike Jannini, Amy McPherson, Julie Moll, and Sid Yu in Bethesda, and so many others who challenged me to apply these concepts to the fascinating and super competitive world of hospitality. My thanks to Pat Stocker, executive development adviser for Marriott, without whose openness, curiosity, and passionate commitment this program would never have happened.

To many colleagues and friends who have shared their ideas about genius, innovation, and customer success, including Jerry Adams, Kevin Beverly, Bob Bookman, Mark Citron, Nancy Coleman, Sherry Conway Appel, Stan Crock, Marc Engel, Stefan Engeseth, Ardell Fleeson, Barbara Friedman, Yoshifumi Fukuzawa, the late Diane Granat, Dave Goodwin, Ruth Hache, Tim Herbst, Lange Johnson, Phil Kiracofe, Rudy Lamone, Melanie Maloney, Virginia Mayer, Gordon Meriwether, Miffy Morgan, Aaron Nierenberg, Robert Nierman, Tim Ogilvie, Tom Paci, Walt Plosila, Jeneanne Rae, Eric Richstein, Becky Ripley, Larry Ross, Cynthia Rubenstein, Herb Rubenstein, Arnold Sanow, Dan Simpkins, Scott Strehl, Randy Wallen, Ann Wilson, and all my friends and colleagues at Leadership Washington, the Boards and partners of Passion for Learning, Inc., and the Primary Care Coalition.

I'd also like to express my sincere appreciation to several people whose insight and inspiration helped me to understand their worlds and the genius in them. Special thanks to Thomas Scalea, Cindy Rivers, Ellen Plummer, Jane Aumick, Jennifer Merenda, Harold Hardinger, Robert Rosenthal, Benjamin

Laughton, and the entire team at the R. Adams Cowley Shock Trauma Center who graciously shared a day in their lives. To John Karas and Ron Paulson at Lockheed Martin who made the world of rocket science come to life. And to Frederick Bigler and his amazing team of concierges at the Ritz-Carlton on Central Park who continually reinvent the notion of delivering compelling value to customers.

I am grateful for the friendship and wisdom of Jordan Lewis, one of the finest people and business minds I have ever had the privilege of knowing. He always brings fresh ideas and even fresher questions to our semi-regular lunches—most often over sushi. In this setting, I have regularly shared my often uncooked ideas and found real guidance and focus.

I will always be indebted to John McKnight, one of my advisers as an undergraduate student at Northwestern University. More than thirty years after I left Evanston, we remain friends, and I continue to be blessed with his compelling wisdom about the potential and the real assets of everyone and every place—especially people and places left outside the mainstream of our society and economy. His thinking is still the most significant learning I have ever received about the genius in all of us and certainly the greatest insight I ever heard on a university campus.

To my agent Nancy Crossman who believed in this project from the start and has always been eager to help me turn my ideas into written words that might matter to others. Even more than being a skilled agent, she is a valued friend.

To my editor Peter Lynch at Sourcebooks who was engaged and thoughtful throughout the process in a way that an author can only hope for. He represents a small but essential group of people in the publishing business who are willing to try new ideas from authors who aren't celebrities. And to the team at Sourcebooks who have been responsive at every step of the way in making sure that this book has had a chance to live up to its potential.

To my publicist Jill Danzig who has been a wonderful partner in promoting this book. Her knowledge, fresh ideas, focus, and upbeat determination have been invaluable in the effort to get the attention of those with influence in the crowded and often confusing world of business books and publicity.

And finally to the most important participants in this or any other endeavor in my life—my family. To my wife, Lisa, who is the most amazing, caring, thoughtful, and inspiring partner anyone could ever have on the journey of life. To our children Sara, Carly, and Noah whose warmth, humor, curiosity, boundless energy, and passion for living are a continuous source of joy and inspiration.

To my parents, Norma and Ed Gregerman, who always instilled in me a desire to travel and make sense of the world and who are still stimulating travel companions on journeys near and far. To my sisters Sandy and Helene Gregerman whose insight, curiosity, questions, and caring will always be an essential part of my life.

Whatever strengths readers find in this book are due in large measure to all of you. The shortcomings are my own.

Index

About the Author

Dr. Alan S. Gregerman is president and chief innovation officer of VENTURE WORKS Inc., a consulting firm based in the Washington, D.C., area that helps leading corporations and organizations to develop winning strategies and create successful new products, services, ventures, and new ways of doing business. His customers are a wide range of Fortune 500 firms, growing companies, entrepreneurial start-ups, and nonprofits, including Discovery Communications, Marriott, Verizon, Lockheed Martin, Raytheon, CitiGroup, Pearson, GlaxoSmithKline, BNA, L3, ICF

International, CGI, Sallie Mae, the Children's National Medical Center, and the National Civil Rights Museum.

Alan is an internationally known expert on strategy, innovation, and differentiation. In the past nineteen years, he has helped more than three hundred teams and organizations to create important innovations—with a 90 percent success rate. He is also an award-winning teacher, author, and public speaker who has been called "one of the most original thinkers in business today" and "the Robin Williams of business consulting." His first book, *Lessons from the Sandbox*, provided a powerful formula for business success based on the magic of childhood. Before starting Venture Works, Alan was the director of entrepreneurial services for a national consulting firm, special assistant for operations at the U.S. Department of Commerce, and the first Visiting Scholar in Entrepreneurship and Innovation at the Library of Congress. He has also worked as a mapmaker and a subway mechanic.

Alan earned his BA in geography, magna cum laude, from Northwestern University. He received his MA in economic geography and PhD in urban and technological planning, with highest honors, from the University of Michigan in Ann Arbor. In his free time, he is founder and president of Passion for Learning, Inc., where he is involved in efforts to build innovative partnerships between the business community and low-income schools to make curriculum come alive for at-risk children. Alan also serves on the board of the Primary Care Coalition and is a math, reading, and writing tutor in the public schools. He and his wife, Lisa, have three children, Sara (14), Carly (9), and Noah (7).

To Learn More

To learn more about speeches, seminars, customized workshops, and consulting services to unlock the genius in your organization and its people, please visit www.venture-works.com. If you would like to contact Alan directly, he can be reached at 301-585-1600 or by e-mail at innovate@venture-works.com.